*Participate joyfully in the sorrows of the world.
We cannot cure the world of sorrows, but we can
choose to live in joy.*

—

JOSEPH CAMPBELL

MATT JONES — @MATT.JONES.PHOTOGRAPHY

OUR MISSION

Modern Huntsman is a publication and media platform for like-minded conservationists, creatives and outdoor enthusiasts. Born out of frustration with the way hunting is often misrepresented in our culture, our objective is to shed light on a more honest side of the story. Told from the perspective of hunting purists and the diplomatically-minded, we present balanced narratives from diverse perspectives to bring about constructive conversations around otherwise controversial topics.

For many of us, hunting is a way of life, a tradition passed down by our grandfathers, fathers and brave mothers. It's a way of staying connected to the land and harvesting wild food to sustain our families, and is a shared passion in most countries the world over. Hunting also plays a major role in conservation, which ensures that wildlife populations thrive and expanses of land stay untamed.

But this isn't just for hunters, and while we know that there will be opposition, we believe that through our collective words, photographs and films, we'll be able to educate some folks about overlooked realities and win the minds and hearts of those who still have them open. Through presenting stories based in virtue and ethics, as well as alternative viewpoints on nuanced or contentious topics, we aim to inspire, educate, challenge, and set the record straight in some cases.

Tired of being spoken against and labeled things we are not, it's time to write a new story about hunting. We created Modern Huntsman to be the banner under which those with common cause can gather, in hopes of finding common ground and sensible solutions.

We hope you'll continue this journey with us.

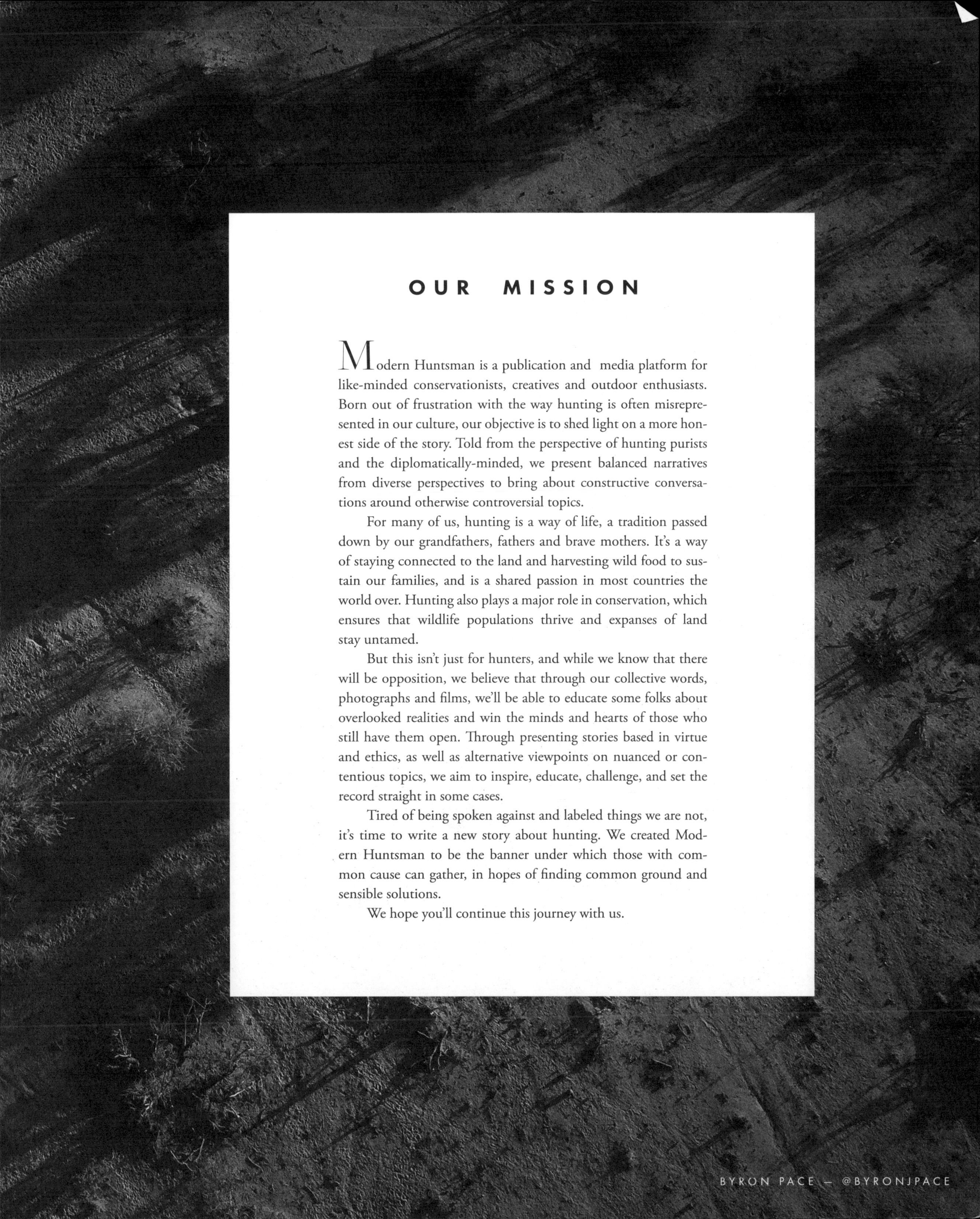

BYRON PACE — @BYRONJPACE

RESILIE

Photo: Frédéric Lagrange

Photo: Stefan Haworth

Photo: Tito West

Photo: Idris Solomon

NCE

CONTRIBUTORS

Sam Averett *@samaverett* Nicholas Coleman *@nicholascolemanart* Chris Douglas *@chrisdouglasphoto* Stefan Haworth *@stefan_haworth* Ryan Holm *@ryan__holm* Rick Hutton *@rhuttonjr* Louise Johns *@e.l.johns* Frédéric LaGrange *@fredericlagrange* Jillian Lukiwski *@thenoisyplume* Lauren Owens Lambert *@lauren.o.lambert* Jonnah M. Perkins *@_.jonnah* Paul Peterson *@paulofthewild_* Idris Solomon *@idrissolomon* Bethany Goodrich *@bethanysgoodrich* D.J. Struntz *@djstruntz* Lailani Upham *@lailani_sue* Dani Verges *@dani_verges* Kiliii Yüyan *@kiliiiyuyan* Laura Zerra *@laurazerra* Emilé Zynobia *@curlsinthewild*

VOLUME SIX

RESILIENCE

KILIII YÜYAN/INSTITUTE — @KILIIIYUYAN

MODERN HUNTSMAN

Printed in Los Angeles by RedCar Media
redcar-media.com

Retailers
modernhuntsman.com/stockist

Contact
info@modernhuntsman.com
modernhuntsman.com
@modernhuntsman

Advertising
modernhuntsman.com/advertise

FRÉDÉRIC LAGRANGE — @FREDERICLAGRANGE

A LETTER FROM TYLER SHARP

EDITOR-IN-CHIEF

"He must put aside his pride, his virtue, beauty and life and bow or submit to the absolutely intolerable."

—

JOSEPH CAMPBELL

Photo of Tyler by Jens Heig after a successful Cape buffalo hunt in Tanzania's Maasailand.

Three years ago when we clicked "launch" on the Modern Huntsman Kickstarter project, I was one rent check away from being bankrupt.

I had just been let go from the only full-time job I've had in the past 15 years, a job that was supposed to make my career as a creative director and allow me to pay off all of the debts that I had accrued in my hard knocks education as a freelancer. I had worked harder for this than anything before — it was supposed to be my big break, but it was taken away faster than you can say "corporate change of initiatives." With it went the financial security, benefits and industry reputation I had so desperately needed.

So I picked up my shattered pride, and the next day went to Elk River Books in Livingston, Montana, and wrote the script for our Modern Huntsman launch film. It was then or never, because what better time to start a print publication and an against-the-current media company than when you're broke, on your ass, and being bet against? One of the biggest disappointments in a long list of failures ended up being the catalyst for one of the best decisions I've ever made.

Here we are now, three years, six books, and over 1,500 pages later. We have accomplished and overcome so much, but it has not been an easy journey. In fact, it's been the most challenging period of my entire life, and there are many days when all the pressure doesn't feel worth it. Sometimes I've wanted to quit.

I have sacrificed so much to keep this going, and have received a lot of personal criticism along the way: I've been called a hipster, a poser, and told that I'm not hardcore enough because I don't fit the mold of what some close-minded individuals think a "hunter" should be. I've lost friends, family members, my freelance career, even the love of my life. I've stood up for contributors, tried to do the right thing, and been thrown under the bus anyway.

Huge opportunities have fallen through, brands have backed out of deals, promises have been broken, and some folks with shallow vendettas have tried their hardest to sabotage the reputation of our brand, and my name. I'm also pretty sure most of my family hasn't read a single word that I've written in these pages.

To be clear, I'm not writing this to complain, or to make you feel sorry for me, but because I recognize these challenges as lessons. These trials have forced me to overcome, to press on, and to be resilient, which is what this issue is all about. All of the strife, loss and tribulation has been worth it, because I truly believe that what we're doing is important, that it will have a lasting impact for generations to come. This thing is worth fighting for, and I am a fighter. I will always get back on the horse.

Whether rebounding from failed projects, broken dreams, or a broken heart, I always push on, try to be better, and face the next challenge bravely. Despite hardships, I have found ways to move forward and become better by learning from mistakes, and by leaning on and trusting the people around me who are good influences. They are sources of inspiration, strength and confidence — my chosen family, many of whom are on this team now.

Why am I telling you this? Perhaps so you'll know a bit more of what we've been through, and where we're headed. More than anything, I hope that it will create some camaraderie, and help you feel closer to the brand, to our team and to me. I don't want this to be a distant and hard-to-reach thing, but rather a community that you feel part of, participate in, and help move forward in your own way. I'd like to know all of you, though it's likely that won't be possible.

Truly, I hope that this resonates in some way, especially given the year that 2020 has turned out to be, and the innumerable challenges that we all have faced. It is for this reason that we did an issue about resilience: to try and remind ourselves and everyone else that we're all capable of so much more than we think. While our struggles might be different, the dynamic human spirit endures in all of us, and we all have the same opportunity to learn from them, grow and persevere. We hope that these stories are a reminder to be resilient, even in challenging times.

In the pages that follow, we have tales of a whale-hunting community that carries on an ancient and beautiful tradition of sustenance, the forgotten history of tough-as-nails Black cowboys in the American West, the miraculous persistence of biodiversity in a modern age of urbanization, survivalists cheating death, the Blackfeet Nation's steadfast reliance on buffalo, and a man who sews seal fur to bring financial aid to a COVID-wracked community in rural Alaska. Of course, in true Modern Huntsman fashion, the stories go much deeper than that.

We're also publishing the winners of our Field Outrider competition, which seeks fresh creative voices and perspectives in an industry that can often feel like an echo chamber. It was an honor to have so many talented judges from all walks of professional life participate, and the caliber of work we received was overwhelming. We'll be commissioning paid assignments with the category winners, which is extremely meaningful to us in a year that has derailed the creative community. Please make sure to meet the winners on page 148, as they all deserve recognition and praise.

A major thank you to our Guest Photo Editor Heidi Volpe, along with her photo team at Patagonia, for all of their efforts in judging the competition, as well as helping curate this issue. We're proud to have them involved, to be able to put outdated industry divisions aside and pursue the greater creative good.

I'd also like to personally thank our very own wonder woman, Miss Katie Marchetti, whose unshakable optimism, hard work and dedication has earned her the new title of Managing Editor. We could not have finished this issue without her, at least not with any shred of grace or poise left. She has been a loyal friend, a fierce defender and a trusted confidant in many dark nights of the soul that this year has dealt. Drop her a note sometime and wish her well; she certainly deserves the acclaim and encouragement.

All that being said, we are very proud to present Volume Six: Resilience, and we hope that these stories are a reminder to be courageous, to rise above and to weather the storm, because much brighter days are on the horizon for all of us. In the words of Christopher Robin, "You are braver than you believe, stronger than you seem, and smarter than you think."

Whether in practice or purpose, aim true and shoot straight.

See you in the field,

Tyler Sharp
Editor-in-Chief | *@tylersharpphoto*

A WORD FROM KATIE MARCHETTI

MANAGING EDITOR

"Never throughout history has a man lived a life of ease and left a name worth remembering."

—

TEDDY ROOSEVELT

It was a perfectly placed shot, well within range, but he didn't fall. While the antelope herd bounded away across the muted plains, the buck stood still. Legs splayed, he wobbled and swayed, nimble hooves firmly planted on the line between this life and the next. Another rifle report granted him peace. I marveled with shaky hands at the resilience of that tough old relic, determined to die on his feet, hoping I too could live with such tenacity.

This year has demanded a great deal of us all, and sometimes when life feels at its darkest we need someone to throw open the window and let in the light — that has been our collective aim for Volume Six. Our hope is that each page rekindles a sense of wonder for wild places; that the collective words and images allow you to marvel at the resilience of the human spirit, and find guiding purpose from the woven complexity of biodiversity.

Despite everything, 2020 forced people to rediscover their need for the great outdoors, valuing wide open places and wildlife like never before. As grocery stores emptied, consumers turned to locally sourced food, protein and veggies planted right down the street. Sourdough loaves were rising in stoves across the globe as people learned to feed themselves by the work of their hands again. When convenience was stricken from our vocabulary, it left room for self-sufficiency to bloom.

Over the years, my family has teased my sister for being a 'cork.' Regardless of the circumstances thrown her way, she always manages to come out on top. Bobbing to the surface, in the face of stormy seas, has little do with our environment and everything to do with what we're made of. We're capable of enduring far more than we've allowed ourselves to believe. Resilience isn't weakened by use, or tripped up by obstacles — it grows stronger with each blow, allowing us to rise with increasing ease, brushing the dust from our jeans.

My hope for you, in the days and pages to come, is that you find renewed hope and your burdens lightened in the knowledge that you're not alone. May you find merit in the foreign and familiar, and may the honest words of a stranger spark a whispered "me too."

I hope you look for the good, and for the green shoots that follow the prune. I hope you're brave enough to believe that people are far more than they seem, and that the only dangerous territory is silencing those with whom you disagree. You have been uniquely placed with a purpose; it matters not whether it has been witnessed by the masses or the mountains. Thank you for sharing your stories, from Cameroon to Idaho, Alaska to the Azores. We've been bolstered by you, and come what may, we will remain.

With resilience and grace,

Katie Marchetti

Katie Marchetti
Managing Editor | *@katiecmarchetti*

A NOTE FROM BYRON PACE

CONSERVATION EDITOR

"Like a symphony of Beethoven, the call of the geese is everlasting, and those who have once known and loved it can never tire of hearing it."

—

MORNING FLIGHT, SIR PETER SCOTT, 1946

When Sir Peter Scott first penned those words in 1935, twenty-six years before he helped found the World Wildlife Fund, he couldn't possibly have fathomed the magnitude of global wildlife decline the following century would witness. A dear friend of Sir David Attenborough, and the grandfather of wildfowling, he embodied the essence of what a naturalist should be. He understood and articulated that human life is richer and more complete in the presence of the other wild beings of this planet. Remove the escalating morning chorus of overhead pinkfeet, or the echoing wrasp of a roaring stag, and my marker of autumn would be lost. The continuum of our mechanized, cyberized world would march on, trampling the life from my body with indifference to their absence. We have to make the conservation of wildlife as integral to our existence as the air we breathe; in the future, we may just realize this as a fundamental truth.

As you read the pages of this volume, you will experience an exploration of human consciousness. Through inexorable love, profound loss, enduring physical feats and physiological contradiction, we present the resilience of our world. As I slowly connected the threads of these stories, settling the gravity of their meaning within my mind, an optimism ensued — a clarity of purpose defined by the resilience I must embrace, for any hope of leaving this place with more than I have taken.

Byron J. Pace

BYRON J. PACE
Conservation Editor | *@byronjpace*

GUEST PHOTO EDITORS

HEIDI VOLPE
&
THE PATAGONIA PHOTO TEAM

Our first zoom chat about the Field Outrider Contest felt like the start of an interesting trip. After a flurry of "Who's in?" texts, the truck was sorta packed, the schedule fuzzy, but the goal clear: bring a variety of creatives together to review work, create community around art, and bridge the gap for more representation and inclusion. The photo team and I wanted to help pave the way for the more seats at the table. It's not about replacing, though. It's about pulling up more chairs.

We were also stoked about this competition because, let's be honest, this year has been awful. Work has been slim to non-existent for many artists. So here was an opportunity to change course and reframe "contest" as guaranteed work for the category winners. And for the judges — well, we never tire of looking at images of folks living their truths and lives fully.

It's our responsibility and honor as photo editors to discover and encourage emerging talent where the photo tells the full story. Thanks for having us along.

Heidi Volpe

HEIDI VOLPE
Director of Photography | *Patagonia*

"You can't wait until you have all the answers before you act."

—

YVON CHOUNIARD
Founder & Chairman | Patagonia

Tumbleweeds of trend are driven by the wind without garnering a second glance, while Tecovas stands firm on western traditions.

Founded by Paul Hedrick, Tecovas provides western goods that impart the comfort and confidence you need to walk tall into new frontiers from the back forty to the boardroom, prairie to penthouse.

Named after a Texas geological formation in Palo Duro Canyon, Tecovas is stubborn about value and uses quality as the guidepost for navigating the rocky terrain and prickly nature of trendy western wear. As we all know, anyone worth their salt has their boots on the ground and eyes on the horizon. Not to be intimidated by sweat-equity, over 200 hand-crafted steps by the artisans of Leon, Mexico go into crafting a single Tecovas boot.

They set out to restore functional art to the western world, yet are on the way to becoming an iconic brand with their rugged Ranch Wear collection. Just as the Vaqueros proudly polished their tools until they saw themselves in it's reflection, Tecovas' sharp-eyed attention to detail will help you find yourself in the perfect pair of boots.

We're honored to work alongside a brand that shoots straight, knows that respect is earned and who are willing to stake their name on quality that will allow you to traverse whatever the trail tosses your way.

TECOVAS

CHRIS DOUGLAS — @CHRISDOUGLASPHOTO

Alone on a mountainside with snow, wind and winter's chill creeping from every corner of the night, Paul Peterson endured.

He was prepared. With First Lite merino wool against his skin, Paul knew that he could rely on his gear to survive the harsh conditions of Idaho's backcountry, and it's why we chose to share his story of resilience in this volume of Modern Huntsman.

First Lite is a stalwart supporter of the hunter, regardless of his or her endeavor. Blending the practical dependability of merino wool with advanced fabric from 37.5 Technology, First Lite garments provide exceptional warmth and moisture wicking capabilities. With a full suite of products designed for sheep hunters like Paul, to whitetail adepts and upland wanderers, there is a head-to-toe solution for the way you want to hunt.

The big picture is not lost in the bottom line, either. First Lite dedicates both time and funds to support organizations that focus on conservation issues like public lands, wildlife preservation and hunter access, for all of these issues are vital for a vigorous outdoor community.

With great uncertainty in our world, we find solace in the leadership and integrity at First Lite.

FIRST LITE

Through collective introspection, the United States is examining the role of blackness in the nation's past, present, and future. We are humbled to have the support of EPIC Provisions as we delve into the rich history of Black cowboys in shaping the legend of the West.

Recognizing the important roles of these men despite tremendous adversity strengthens the understanding of Western identity at this pivotal point in history.

Perhaps more than ever, people are examining where their food comes from and scrutinizing the idea of nourishment. A growing number of ranchers are implementing management techniques that fall into the regenerative agriculture movement, which celebrates the natural, primal relationship between animals, soil, and people. EPIC Provisions seeks to support human health, animal health, and the land through products that can be incorporated into everyday life.

Grass-fed protein and spices provide the foundation for EPIC Bars, and their approach to sourcing those ingredients gives farmers and ranchers incentive to improve their land while raising high-quality products. The goal is to eat with the land.

EPIC PROVISIONS™

IDRIS SOLOMON — @IDRISSOLOMON

This year, everyone has been tested.

As a nation, as individuals, forces beyond our control checked the fabric of our resiliency. When the pandemic reached the doors of MYSTERY RANCH, the talented men and women set aside the pack designs and got to work making masks for those who needed them most: medical professionals in their community who faced covid-19 every single day.

Dana Gleason, the godfather of pack design, and his partner Renee Sippel Baker have been working together for over 40 years to create a heritage of unmatched quality and durability in their packs. A distillation of time, space, and unwavering dedication to the task at hand, MYSTERY RANCH continues to be the standard of unprecedented strength and comfort today.

Those who choose a MYSTERY RANCH pack also rise to the challenge before them: the firefighter who battled unrelenting blazes across the West; the medic whose duty is to enter harm's way and save the lives of their countrymen; the hunter who pushes their limits for an honorable hunt.

Together, as we face the challenges of tomorrow, we are humbled by MYSTERY RANCH's steadfast support to our mission.

MYSTERY RANCH

RYAN HOLM — @RYAN_HOLM

You can't hunt what you can't see.

Which is why Vortex optics are dedicated to providing the finest rugged optics so you can have a clear view of what's ahead. Since 1986 Vortex has been an American-owned, Veteran-owned, family-owned-and-operated business, which Dan and Margie Hamilton turned into one of the top manufacturers of outdoor optics today.

With unconditional and unlimited VIP warranty, this Wisconsin company stands by their promise to put people first.

Vortex has the foresight to provide the tools for you to cover more ground with your eyes than with your feet. Saving the legs of avid outdoorsmen one exceptionally clear, colorful and crisp picture at a time. Whether you're entering foreign or frontier territory, rising to the challenge means utilizing superhuman vision, precision, perseverance and resilience.

Vortex provides the first two, the rest is up to you.

VORTEX®

RICK HUTTON — @RHUTTONJR

1995
PRESENTED BY — CHRISTENSEN ARMS

25 YEARS

CHRISTENSEN ARMS

CELEBRATES THEIR SILVER ANNIVERSARY

Words by BILL RODEN

I come from humble beginnings, and there's an old saying in my family: "We're too poor to buy cheap." This tenet was usually reserved for everyday workhorse essentials like vacuum cleaners and snow shovels. On a waning afternoon on the last day of a frigid late-season hunt in Colorado back in 2008, this credo lingered as we hunkered down behind a natural blind 200 yards away from an elusive pair of cow elk. My friend had recently purchased a .300 Win Mag just for this hunt from a company that shall remain nameless out of respect. This rifle was an entry-level, hammer-fired platform that many owners hot-rod with aftermarket parts. Following pseudoscience forum advice, my friend added a heavier hammer and hammer extender. With the wind working in our favor, we set up for his opportune shot, locked on to a healthy cow, and my friend pulled the hammer back. Then we both heard an audible snap that seemed to reverberate across the canyons. In that rare moment, when the cosmos pulled everything together for us, my friend's hammer and extender sheared clean off, rendering his rifle as useful as a makeshift club. At that moment, his eyes widened into dinner plates and broadcast the same stunned gaze of a bull rider bucked under 2,000 pounds of testosterone as he grasps the true gravity of the situation in slow motion. Two ungulate noses, each with over 300 million olfactory receptors and powered by a sixth sense, lifted into the air and disappeared into the aspen on high alert.

We laugh about it now around the campfire while one-upping each other with yarns about epic hunts gone sideways. All those weekends away from family spent scouting and marking maps. All those scorching-hot days and dollars spent getting dialed in at the range in the high desert. The hours at the gym; the night my friend slept on the couch after his wife eye-balled pricey binos and a winter layering system on the credit card bill. All of the time, money, sacrifice and energy we exhausted preparing for my friend's first elk hunt ended with a minute sound that remains forever in my ears. In that instant, our family doctrine proved itself true yet again.

Meanwhile, one state over in Gunnison, Utah, the women and men of Christensen Arms were hard at work crafting rifles that reimagined every inch of a firearm from the ground up, so that you don't have to. They concept, design and build hard-use rifles in-house that incorporate aerograde materials like carbon fiber and titanium under the critical eyes of former aerospace engineers. In the fall of 2020, Christensen Arms celebrated their 25th anniversary — a significant milestone when you consider the intense competition and the fragmented and entrenched subcultures within the firearms world, and an unforgiving audience quick to jettison high-end brands if they fall short even once. As you look past Christensen Arms' legendary firearms and make your way through their brand and company, one word comes to mind: balance.

Precision and balance are table-stakes when it comes to premium firearms, but 'balance' takes on deeper dimensions in the world of Christensen Arms. They craft true shooter's rifles, but spend the necessary time working with new shooters to provide the purpose-built firearms they need, not just what they think they need. They apply the world's most innovative materials, normally reserved for satellites and fighter jets, with old-world attention to detail and customer service. They employ and continue to train expert craftsmen in the industry, but reserve those cherished jobs for the very town they started in, never forgetting their humble beginnings in Roland Christensen's garage. They put customers, employees and their families first and their stellar products a close second. Christensen Arm builds rifles with the biggest hearts.

Founders Roland and Jason Christensen are aerospace engineers with a long history of building prosthetic limbs and other meaningful products using the very same materials and techniques they put into every firearm. All of this is bound together by Julia Christensen, a supportive mom, wife, friend and family rock who never wavered from her family's lofty mission to build the world's most accurate, lightweight rifles in America. A family business to this day, what began in their garage quickly scaled to a meticulous operation that caters to professional shooters, hunters, celebrities and demanding owners alike. Originally pioneers of carbon fiber barrels, they ushered in an era of lightweight, high-performance rifles that opened up more terrain and greater distances for shooters and hunters. Each piece earns it keep; when you find it outperforms custom firearms right out of the box, modifications aren't mandatory. Starting with 25 rifles a month, they've upgraded to over 1,000 due to proven demand. Every build leaves the shop having passed through many proud, callused hands. Each employee I've spoken with exudes a sense of pride with an explorer's sense of wonder as they continue to challenge the sacred cows of the industry. Christensen Arms doesn't waiver from their core technology and company values. Jeff Bradley, an Christensen Arms team member, recently stated, "One of my favorite things to hear from a customer is that they have many rifles, but the majority are Christensen Arms. When your brand is lucky enough to be in a gun safe more than once, we feel that says something and we don't take it for granted. Our production and assembly team handles each firearm, knowing that it has to be worthy of the "that's-a-Christensen-Arms-rifle" reputation we have built. Our production and assembly teams never want to hear anything different, so every firearm piece is handled with the utmost care and pride." There's a characteristic feel-in-hand when you pick up a Christensen Arms rifle that proves out their ethos. The feeling of innovative design brought to life through advanced materials and machining is on par with the visceral feeling one gets when stepping into a luxury car for the first time. Their MPR rifle recently won 2020 Rifle of the Year. Yet every rifle they make has the right amount of familiarity that's simple to dial-in for pros and novices alike. Christensen Arms is equally at home both in high-end gun safes and national retailers. This makes their rifles the perfect companion for anyone embarking on a late-season elk hunt in Colorado.

Customers shop differently these days, putting greater pressure on firearm companies to adapt at the speed of the fickle consumer. Barrel whip, stiffness, and how much nickel is incorporated into the steel are now on an equal consideration plane as to how well a company treats its people and overall customer service. Many manufacturers are buckling under the pressure to innovate while developing greater community management. Everything a company does talks. A few giants of the industry have fallen as a result, while people-first brands like Christensen are moving at breakneck speed to take their place.

After 25 years in an industry and culture that has seen a monumental amount of change in both culture and product advancements, Christensen Arms is just getting started. New innovations like their Modern Precision Rifle are indicators that listening to their consumers, not the industry, is setting the talented people of Gunnison, Utah on a course to become not only a great American firearm brand, but one of America's next great brands overall. Wherever they go, many are sure to follow — consumers and competitors alike.

CHRISTENSEN ARMS®

2020

BILL RODEN

PRESENTED BY — **CHRISTENSEN ARMS**

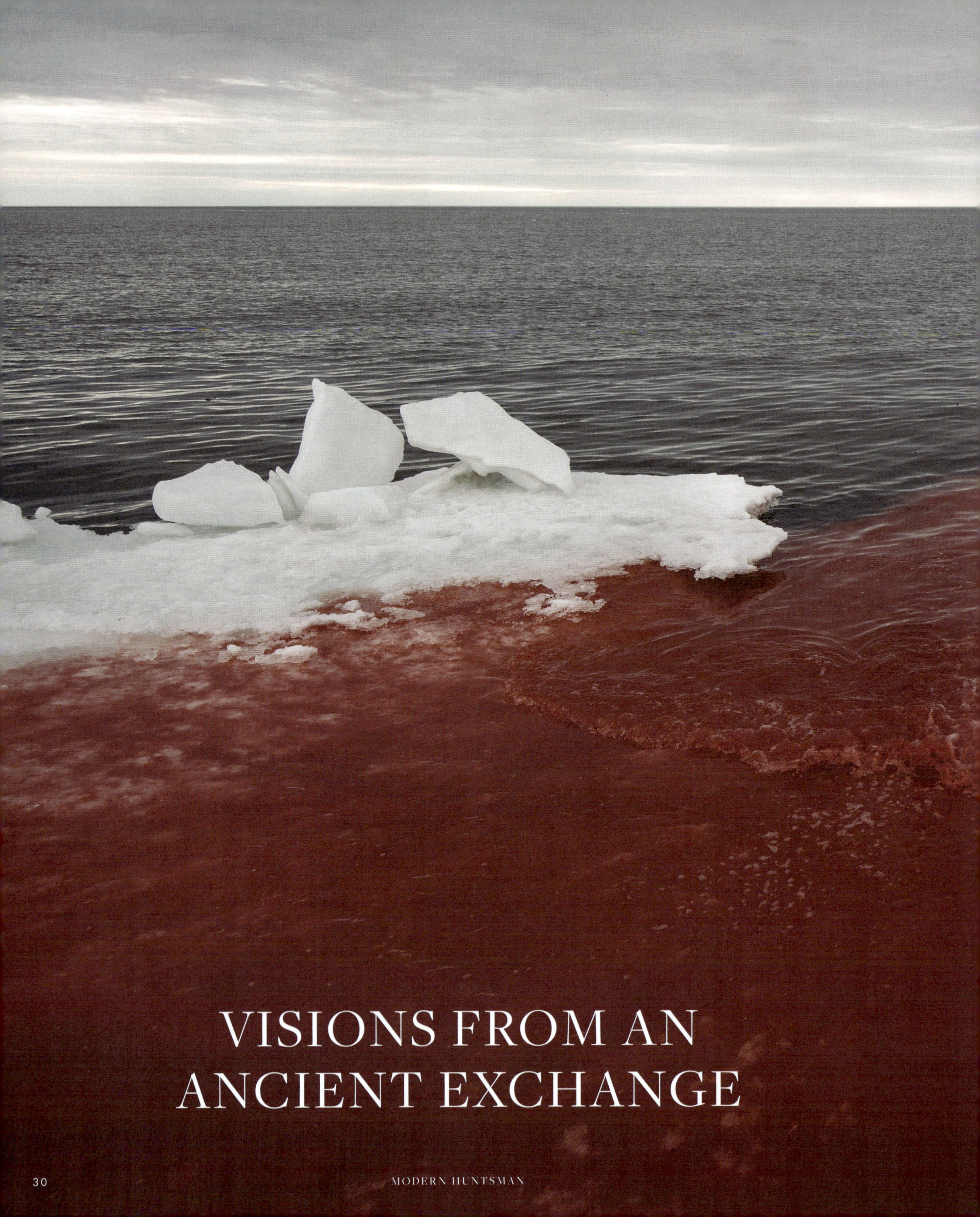

VISIONS FROM AN ANCIENT EXCHANGE

Words by JACK EVANS *Photos by* KILIII YÜYAN/INSTITUTE

Hide something for me.
Look at the food, the whales. Look at the sea, the whalers.
A blessing for them.

Take that and hide it in your heart.

—

FOSTER SIMMONDS, Iñupiat Elder

Utqiaġvik is a small community, locked in ice for all but a few weeks a year at the northmost edge of America. The people there, the Iñupiat, live by the flat ocean, through nightless summers and long, aurora-lit winters. When the seasons tilt during two brief months in spring and fall, thousands of whales — bowhead and beluga — navigate along their shores. Here is where the Iñupiat launch boats built from sealskins, driftwood and the other gifts that float to their world's white edge. They catch the bowhead whales with hand-thrown harpoons, hauling in a dozen or more and eating from the *maktak*, the blubber, that they drag off the animals in heavy blocks. They celebrate this bounty with the whole of their symbology, their identity, and leave only bloody bones for the polar bears to climb and chew. From one of the largest animals ever known on this Earth — from its body, its great herdlike society and its monumental intelligence — the Iñupiat create their own lifeway and thrive.

This is a harvest of the largest animals hunted today. Bowheads stretch to sixty feet and more (the size of a semi-trailer). In the thousands, they swim from an unknowable ocean up to the same frozen shore on their long journeys around the Pacific world. The oldest among them will remember Utqiaġvik when it was a cluster of sod houses before it was considered "America," as well as the days when it was called "Barrow." Whales will live to see what future human generations make of the place.

Some 2,500 Iñupiat, standing on that shore, know them best. The hunt is a relationship created between these people and the whales, an ancestral tradition still-enacted while the ice slowly melts, and in its abundance, risk, poetics and lessons, the Iñupiats form their ever-evolving, gorgeous and dangerous existence.

The scope of just how much this ocean hunt shapes human lives on the Northern Shore is difficult to comprehend from any distance. Kiliii Yüyan is the journalist who's lived at the keenest edge of the great encounter for five seasons running. *Modern Huntsman* sat down with him to decipher the frames of meaning made out on the water's surface. Where the whale's world briefly meets our own, transfers of life, death, dreams and gifts define a vitally unique way of modern human life.

Kiliii is a photographer and a spring season whaling crew-member. The line between his artwork and hunt-work is willfully blurred. Informed by knowledge from Nanai/Hezhe (Siberian Native), Chinese and American ancestry, Kiliii seeks a story educated by multiple viewpoints — or none at all. A hunt, in a moment, cannot be foretold.

Today, this is how the Iñupiat live and thrive from the world's heaviest harvest.

KILIII YÜYAN: Western logic has this sort of weird, strict, 'civilized' assumption that humans are destructive to nature. Animals are separate and not compatible, and if humans inhabit a wilderness, nature will suffer.

That is not the assumption of the Iñupiat.

I cannot speak for them. I can only give my perspective on how I understand what people have told me, the feelings they've relayed to me. The Inupiat consider the ocean to be their garden. They say: "This is our garden. We take care of our garden." And when you think about a wilderness, even an ocean, in that way, the relationship is very different. That means that they're caretaking that place and have a relationship with all the beings in it — the opposite of this notion that there's some kind of pristine nature that can only thrive when left alone. They don't know of a nature that's separate from humanity.

I think that we still, as Westerners — or any heavily modernized, globalized people — have a strong inclination to think that the land is somehow better off without humans in it. We seem to think it's better off unmodified, without ever realizing that everything that you see in the wild has become pristine and beautiful because some Indigenous communities somewhere took care of it for several thousands of years to create it that way.

For example, one year, the International Whaling Commission created a moratorium on bowhead hunting that lasted for a season. It didn't go over very well. U.S. Government scientists went up there to count the whales. They basically said: "There's a whale going by on the ice. That's one." They counted 800 whales across the North Slope in this way. That's obviously not a sustainable number for hunting, so they declared a moratorium on it. All the Iñupiat elders told them, "You're off by an order of magnitude. You're totally wrong."

Not long afterward, a government scientist named Craig George developed a new system where they used acoustic sounding and advanced statistics to count bowheads more accurately. There ended up being 8,000 whales, a tenfold increase, and pretty much exactly the number that the elders had said. Everyone was stunned, and that was when management passed to Indigenous hands, to what's now the Alaska Eskimo Whaling Commission.

None of the Iñupiat hunters I've spoken with think about conservation on this grand scale, but that doesn't mean that they don't have a powerful cultural framework that ensures the survival of wildlife populations. The way they talk about it, worldview and perspective all depends on your relationships, your experience.

When you're out there whaling, you're standing on ice floating on top of the Arctic Ocean. You're huddled behind some windbreak at the edge, where the ice meets the water. That's where the whales come by, and that's where they get harpooned. The skin boats that you have, *umiaqs*, get pushed from the ice into the water very quickly. You never chase a whale if you're going to get wet — you try really hard not to get wet up there — so it's then just a couple of paddle strokes until you're alongside it. It's essentially an ambush hunting style.

But sometimes whales will pass by and hunters won't pursue them. Often that's because it's easy to lose the whale in the weather conditions; or, it's for other reasons that are much more subtle and difficult to explain. One of the things that opened my eyes the most was a moment when I was sitting on the edge of the ice, on watch, and I spotted a whale swimming very close to us. It was moving slow and it all looked perfect — the right size and age — so I ran back and woke the captain. It was the middle of the night, daylight, and he just poked his head out of the tent and looked at the whale for a moment.

Then he said, "Oh, that one's not for us. That one hasn't chosen us."

In my head I thought, What? You just glanced at it!

He said, "Oh just watch, just watch."

Six or seven minutes went by, and I completely forgot about it — I was just zoned out and watching for whales again. But then I saw that the crew a few hundred yards away from us had woken up their captain as well. The whale that we had seen before came up to them. It surfaced in front of their boat and just lay there and slowly rolled, showing its back — two or three rolling motions right in front of their *umiaq*. So they pushed the *umiaq* out and harpooned it, and my captain turned to me and said, "It chose them."

The first thought in my head was: this is not a metaphor.

* * *

When a crew makes a strike and they have successfully landed a whale, the call always goes out over the radio: "Blessings for the whale and thank you for a gift." Then there's usually a chorus of cheers. People say, "Ye-he-he!," which comes from the old European whalers, and then, "aarigaa" which means "very good."

The other thing that's interesting is that when they bring it onto land, there's a person who will come and stand there with his arms out — a gesture of thanks to the whale. I've seen it many times. I don't know where it comes from, whether that's a Christian symbol, being like a cross, or something much older, but it's still a "thank you" to the whale.

Even before you go out whaling, the whole crew gets together and an elder like my friend, Foster Simmonds, comes and says a prayer:

"Hide something for me. Look at the food, the whales. Look at the sea, the whalers. A blessing for them. Take that and hide it in your heart."

* * *

Becoming a whaler is like an apprenticeship; no one really explains much. You figure it out by watching. All the whalers in my crew started when they were six, so they've been watching and learning for at least ten years. They become really useful around their teenage years. When they're strong, they start clearing ice trails or working the blocks and tackle used to pull whales up. For four months of the year, including the spring and fall seasons, the whalers are hunting. Essentially, that's a third of their life.

From that comes a lot of individual innovation — not in terms of technology, but rather in technique, which depends on your particular perception and understanding of the whale. A lot of the evolving knowledge comes from deep, communal observation.

There's a fascinating aspect about this that I've observed the whole time: every one of these crews has an old-school VHF radio that they use to communicate with each other. There's constant chatter, but it's seldom personal. Mostly it's just observations that are spoken over the radio. Now, as a journalist, I would occasionally ask a question that was difficult to answer. The individual hunter would sometimes know, but if they were really interested in the question, they would ask it into the VHF radio. They wouldn't tell me anything themselves — it would just disappear into the VHF. Later I would hear side chatter around this question. The hunters would add observations around it. Then, a couple of days later, usually after I'd forgotten about it, I would get an answer.

It was like putting a question into a black box and seeing what came out. There's actually a book that studies this, called *The Whale and the Supercomputer* (by Charles Wohlforth). The theory in the book is that the whalers' VHF radio works like a neural network. A huge amount of observations go into it, and a single hunter — a node of the network — won't process them alone. But the collected minds think about it and eventually decide an answer.

I think that's partly because Iñupiat are not big on giving definitive answers to things — that's not what you do when you're truly observing. You're hunting, and the questions about the whales are always there. Where are they? What are they doing? When will we see them? Why? You're always revising your understanding based on new observations. You don't want to be a hundred percent definitive on things, which is that same issue that scientifically minded people have with their kind of knowledge.

The VHF radio is fascinating and constant. You hear people chattering over it about what's going on in the sea and all these whale movements, but I don't think I ever heard a definitive statement about anything. And it was great! I learned to really appreciate listening to the observations all the time.

Even though I've been up there for the spring season for five years now, it's not enough to understand some of the things they talk about, like the subtleties of where a harpoon strike should land. Sometimes I'll hear clear observations — "We just had a strike" — but there are a lot of statements like: "A whale has come up to help another whale." There's no interpretation offered for that. I eventually learned that there were good reasons not to interpret, because you'd hear the same story a couple of days later, but it would be totally different. From "A whale is floating there and all the other whales have passed it by," you can draw many different conclusions, so in a way, each might be wrong. It's fascinating, the decision not to firmly, absolutely know. It's humility before nature. And it keeps you observing, paying attention.

* * *

Sometimes I would find myself searching for my own, naturally biased interpretations, but when the hunting with the VHF really comes together, you just stop asking hard questions. You turn off your prefrontal cortex — the part that's doing all the interpreting and answering of questions — and get into the mode of simply inputting data, observing and watching what's going on.

When I'm on watch and I've been there for a couple of hours, it's like I'm not inside my body. Like my tendrils have reached out to the distant horizon. My peripheral vision is picking up different bits of information and it's all just moving and flowing around me. It feels like I get it. I can understand how the light part of the clouds over there means that the floating ice pack far away is coming toward us, which explains why I'm seeing more whales close by, which explains why the belugas are here. All of these different things are interacting with each other and I don't need to have my mind in it. I'm just feeling and pulling it all in.

* * *

There are all kinds of gestures of respect toward the whales. Whenever I was in an ice cellar, people would tell me that if you don't keep your cellar clean, the whale won't give itself to you. Whales don't like dirty ice cellars. It's a sign of respect, but it also serves the pragmatic purpose of ensuring that people don't waste *maktak*, that no one accumulates more than they need.

Another thing that you see a lot is how adherence to tradition differs between the crews. My crew is very strict about always wearing our white, ice-camouflage whaling parkas when we're on watch close to the edge of the ice. The whale's underwater, and far away, so they're not really going to see you, but that was a powerful belief of my crew captain. You aren't allowed to drive snow machines anywhere close to the edge of the ice, make sudden movements, or ever wear red.

I don't think these things are superstitions, though. I think they come from direct, individual relationships with hunted and remembered whales.

Maybe the most you can explain about those parts of their belief is through stories. One elder, Harry Brower Sr., who was immensely well respected before he died, was pivotal in the creation of the Eskimo Whaling Commission and all the indigenous decision-making systems that it established. At one point, they had this issue with the hunts: how do we avoid hunting pregnant whales? Killing a pregnant whale has been a sort of taboo, but it still occasionally happened. Harry was in a hospital in Anchorage when he dreamed that a baby whale visited him, and he had this vision of it being killed by hunters he knew, back in Utqiaġvik. It turned out that it had actually happened. Harry even named the exact ice cellar where that whale's meat was stored. This baby whale in the dream, though, told Harry the prohibitions they needed to establish to protect the carrying mothers. Because of that, the spring whaling season deadline was set around their pregnancies — it's still observed, and the whale population has risen.

So again, conversations with the animals and the spirit world are recognized in these direct ways. They have real effects. These understandings could be based on a simple moral prerogative, and I don't know how much of that recognition is altered by their Christian beliefs, but it seems unimportant. Whether that describes a purely animistic kind of belief or a hybrid of different things, it doesn't matter — this is just what the people see.

The struggle with contradiction is something that is more characteristic of the Western mind. Western thinking relies heavily on logic — linear and cause-and-effect thinking — and isolating variables. Science is very powerful in that way. Still, it doesn't contradict the ideas of the Iñupiat, their mindset. They integrated Christianity when it arrived, and still can understand this animistic dream-communication. They don't make much of a distinction between an individual animal, a species, or the spirit version of that animal. But they also don't see a contradiction in hunting individual whales and saving the species.

The hunters fluidly move back and forth between the killing and the loving sides of the relationship. After a whale is brought onto the shore, other crews will go up and touch the whale and hang out with it, feel it. Then they'll gather and talk about how good of a harpoon strike it was.

* * *

So people ask this all the time: how can hunting help to save the whale? Taking a purely rationalist perspective on it does make that harder. One way to describe it is that as you hunt the whale, you have a relationship with it. You occupy that human side of the relationship, and you depend on it. You've created an interdependency, and because you occupied that space, nobody else can. So if outsiders bent on resource extraction come in and are thinking about the whale as a resource, not a being to relate to, then it's easier to keep them out.

Still, in the last ten years, we've seen an increasing presence of the oil and gas industry, and with it the very American idea of progress for the sake of progress. Hunters talk to me about how they don't want to go backward. One man was telling me: "The caribou are sick; they come in with these lumps in their fat that we can't identify. Sometimes the fish from around the oil wells are sick and have sores on them. But we don't want to give up oil and gas drilling altogether. We don't want to go back to living in sod houses."

So you have this back-and-forth questioning going on, and there's a lot of tension in the political atmosphere. It's like a wedge being driven into the communities and villages by oil and gas.

The Iñupiat would never want to lose whaling, though. It's very much at the center of who they are. Whale symbolism is everywhere, and the hunting relationship is the core of the community. Along with language, it's a primary part of their identity. What's unfortunate is that climate change will be the thing that ends the traditional hunts.

The sea ice is the platform for the boats to ambush the whales from. That sea ice is retreating, closer and closer to the land — the 'fast ice.' Eventually it will melt away to the shore, and it won't be possible to hunt with *umiaqs* in the traditional way. Whaling can carry on by motorboat, where hunters drive out and chase the whales around. The young guys really like to do that, whereas the older guys prefer the quieter, traditional technique.

The *umiaq* is sewn out of fermented seal skin, around a frame of driftwood. If you stop using *umiaqs*, what do you do with the skins of the bearded seals? If you don't need the skins, then you stop hunting the seals, and then no one has any relationship with the seals anymore. If that's lost, the seals will still be swimming around, but the intentionally created interdependence that currently exists on a large scale? That's really hard to organically re-establish once it's gone.

Still, whaling will go on in some way even as the sea-ice retreats. I think the most unfortunate thing about it, though, is that the long-created interdependence slowly gets chipped away at by these modern changes. Future Iñupiat may look back on their ancestors, hunting whales with motorboats, saying "that's not traditional!" But who would remember how to build an *umiaq*? That's the danger when the memory of a people gets replaced.

I don't think that anyone's really imagined stopping hunting, though. I don't think I've ever heard anyone even speculate on that — it's just mind-blowing to them. Whaling has been going on for the entirety of their known history.

The year before I arrived for my first season, some scientists found an old scar on a whale that some Iñupiat had harvested. One reached in and pulled out this strange harpoon head. They stared at it until they realized it was made of stone.

"How old is this? Nobody has used stone for at least 160 years!" The elders had been saying that the whales lived for 200 years, but the scientists didn't believe them. That would make them some of the oldest living mammals on Earth — and indeed, they are. Scientists eventually figured out how to age whales based on rings in their retinas and showed that the oldest bowhead harvested was 212 years old.

How did the elders know that? I'm not entirely sure, but I think it lies in a combination of talking about things, every detail, for generations of hunting, and also personally remembering specific whales, specific encounters and passing that down.

The oral historians of the community remember stuff from 50 years ago like it was yesterday. There's no doubt to me that some of this knowledge is kept in the same way that VHF works — communally.

* * *

I was on the ice once when a pregnant whale was hauled in. That can still happen, by anomaly or accident. She had a fourteen-foot baby inside her. Some scientists were with us, and they were thrilled because they can only study bowheads when they've been harvested by Iñupiat, and they rarely get a chance to study a baby. But I was there when they cut it open and this baby came out. Everyone was stunned and stood still. For about a minute, no one could say anything. There were maybe a hundred people on the ice and everyone was just in this wave of silence — it spread out.

Honestly, I was just feeling what everyone else was feeling. I would say I was feeling emotion secondhand, absorbing the group's energy. And then I closed my eyes for a few seconds, and it just all kicked in. That sense or state of gratitude and sadness at once.

That contradiction, I feel like, is a lot easier for me, perhaps more than for any of my neighbors here in Seattle, because I'm a hunter and a fisherman. When I see these things happening, personally, I feel joy. I feel joy that Indigenous communities are able to carry on the instructions of their ancestors, in all their complexity. And while I'm never thinking this in the moment, this is a purposeful encounter, deeply driven inside of me, that I already know. So I feel the sorrow, but I have an understanding that at some point in time, the animals and humans got together and made an agreement — an agreement that the hunter has with its hunted, which is that you don't take the body of the hunted in vain. You do it for a reason — to feed people, to live. I get the sense that all hunting's like this. This is the ancient agreement that goes way back to the ancestors, of the whale and the hunters as well. That agreement is being fulfilled. And that is a beautiful thing. That is a wonderful thing. That's a thing to feel joy for.

FACING PAGE "On one of my first days out on the sea ice — I'll never forget — we had a polar bear attack. All of a sudden I heard Robert screaming: *'Nanuk! Nanuk!'* Everyone went quiet and just started looking around. When I finally saw it, I realized that my eyes were looking too far out on the horizon. It was right there, fifteen yards from me. You never go anywhere without a rifle there, but of course this was the one unguarded moment that we were just setting up camp. I saw Larry, to my left, looking through his pockets for bullets. Meanwhile, the polar bear is pushing off of its front haunches because it had been laying down on the ice so we couldn't see it. He probably had his nose covered also. He starts to push off, moving forward, getting his momentum going. Then I see one of the guys on the right sliding towards the rifle, grabbing it and swinging around to shoot all in one motion. The polar bear hasn't even gotten completely off the ground yet and it gets hit right in the spine. He falls and skids, maybe a couple of feet. And then we skinned it. It was a huge bear, it would have been eleven feet standing, but it was skinny, and when we opened its mouth we saw that two out of the four canine teeth were broken. No apex predator wants to attack eight men, but being so hungry it was desperate enough to try anyway."

P.30-31 One of my favorite photographs is of a wave washing in over the top of the ice from the ocean, and the wave is just red. It's a bloody wave, quite beautiful because it's frozen in time and all there is around it is ice. It's happened because we've harvested a whale and its blood is mixing with an unusual current. I don't ever really share this one outside of a fine art context, where interpretation is much more ambiguous, but when I show that to Iñupiat, they seem to know exactly what it means to them. They look at it and they feel a sense of joy. They'll say: 'Our tradition is continuing; this is who we are. This is what it was like to be out there. Peace.' Whereas if I show it to just about anyone else, they're afraid! It makes them think of mortality — and not even necessarily their own mortality, but death in general, and in fear of it.

P.32-33 The main cemetery in Utqiaġvik is where many Iñupiat ancestors lie. Most Iñupiat families are Christian and have been for three generations and more. People visit their ancestors here all the time.

P.34 Sometimes you might see 200 bowheads pass by over the course of a day and some days you might only see three. It's the bowhead migration that we hunt, though — a herd type hunt. Whales only get harpooned at a maximum of a hundred yards off the ice, because the *umiaq* skin boats we have get pushed into the water and it's only a couple of paddle strokes before we're on the whale. So it's essentially an ambush hunting style.

P.36-37 The harpoon is thrown and it immediately curves downwards, making for a solid downward thrust with weight. The harpoon head goes into the whale through the skin and toggles off, leaving it attached to the harpoon line. Behind the harpoon head is a trigger for a tiny explosive rocket, which fires down into the whale and detonates, hopefully killing the whale quickly and humanely, and creating less danger for the crew as well.

P.41 This is the old gesture that's made every time a whale is pulled up. These gestures of respect are all part of Iñupiat society. I think I feel a particular joy for being a part of this hunt because it's the kind of thing that the rest of the world is actively trying to get rid of.

P.42-43 In any given season there are about fourteen or fifteen whales taken for the village. When the first whale of a season is caught the whole village comes to pull it up. Once they've butchered the main chunks and brought it in, each of the 37 crews gets a share. The meat from the jaws is the best part, so that gets divided and apportioned. What's interesting is that crews will then send pieces out to their relatives, and this network goes far beyond the village. People will fly with the whale on the Alaska Airlines flight down to Portland, to Seattle, or ship it in a cooler. There are literally thousands of pounds of whale meat going out every year to all the different family members in their network.

P.44 A lot of the whalers identify with the bears, or *nanuk* — as hunters, obviously, but also as survivors. They admire the endurance that bears have, to live in the same Arctic conditions. Plus, they're innovative, like humans. The hunters actually really liked to let the *nanuk* eat from the whales. One time we had a big beast of one come down, with this huge scar on its head. It was like a monster arriving, and you could hear some of the guys murmuring: 'Oh, he's a *survivor*. Let him eat!'

P.46 Here, a boy is picking out a piece of seal blubber out of a jar of fermented seal oil. The oil is all that is left after the fat begins to ferment, and is used as a dipping oil or poured over the precious few inland greens harvested in the summer.

P.47 This is inside of my whaling crew's shop, the outbuilding where the hunt preparations are made. The window is small and triple-paned for insulation. The bear skulls are from polar bears that the crew has taken over the last 50 years, including the one that attacked my crew.

P.48-49 Because of climate change, the sea ice is getting so thin that it becomes impossible to pull the whales up on top of it. It's been five years now, and I'm still covering the "story," but I'm no longer going there with very specific questions to solve. I go because I'm part of the community! The crew needs to be able to count on me, and it's my one time a year to hang out with my friends there. But I certainly still have open... inquiries. I photograph it because I find that I learn a lot more through my work as a photographer. I'm interested in their world, and photographing it is like giving myself express permission to inquire, and to seek out understandings that aren't natural to me. The Iñupiat understand and constantly practice this hunt, with all its knowledge. Coming with a camera gets them to share it with me.

Story by JILLIAN LUKIWSKI

WE ARE WHAT WE EAT

"Until we understand what the land is, we are at odds with everything we touch."

—

WENDELL BERRY

We have returned home to our farm after a successful elk hunt in the high country. It was cold at ten thousand feet, the land already transformed by the wheels of autumn spinning at maximum velocity — disrobed aspen trees, freezing nights, and ice on the spring creek in camp every morning. It was a different world. It is late October on the farm, and we have yet to feel the icy grip of a killing frost. The edges of our land are brilliant with fall hues as the trees begin to give up their leaves. My garden has remained lush, colored with an array of flowers, ripe vegetables, and bushes of bright herbs. This has been the longest growing season of my life, a miraculously gentle Indian summer. I lift my face to a bluebird sky, I feel the wind and sun and energy of the day, and I give thanks.

I was raised on homegrown produce and began helping my mother in the garden at the age of three or four. She and her five sisters were raised on a wheat farm in Saskatchewan, where they grew their own food along with a few thousand acres of grain. My mother taught me the same skills she learned as a little girl and impressed upon me a specific set of values: work hard, grow as much of your own food as you are able to, waste little, make do. Everywhere my husband and I have lived in our sixteen years of marriage — Alaska, Arizona, Idaho, Washington — we have grown a portion of our food. In Alaska, I used our outhouse with its corrugated clear plastic roof to grow a bumper crop of bell peppers. I treated the john like a greenhouse, and while visitors were suspicious of my bathroom decor choices, those peppers were as delicious as they were innovative. Everywhere we have called home has a similar gardening story. We had some dirt. We did some planting and tending. We ate the fruit of our labor. A few years ago, we purchased a modest working farm in a temperate river valley and so began our farming career.

Our farm is a bantam-sized operation; you won't find monocropped miles of corn or wheat here. The majority of our land is put to orchard hay, which is mowed and baled by a neighbor and taken to market. Our leftover acreage is committed to livestock enclosures, fruit and nut orchards, a massive home garden, a sizable garlic plot that undergoes yearly expansion, and a lawn studded with seventy mature trees which help dilute the heat of summer in the high desert. Our farm is an oasis. We have water rights to a portion of the Snake River and we grow our food in robust volcanic soil beneath a fevered sun. We are diversified and will continue to diversify our livestock and our niche market crops. We sell our hay and our garlic locally, supported by members of our community. We are generalists. We keep many irons in the fire. When we experience failure, we look for another way. We never give up. We're farmers.

Every year brings four new seasons to test new ideas, raise different livestock, grow new plant varieties, and attempt antiquated food storage techniques. We apply our minds and our muscles to our work, and our land is a thoughtful and consistent teacher. When I look out at what we have built, I can see that the strength of our humble operation relies on the health of our soil, which depends on our community of livestock as well as our general treatment of the ecosystem we have built here. We believe that a single species does not make an ecosystem and similarly, one thousand acres of wheat does not make a farm. It takes the interaction of many species to build a healthy, resilient biome, and we are trying our best to model this belief as we design our farmscape and develop it in new directions each year. Successful small farming hinges on our ability to remain attentive to the needs of our soil instead of simply enslaving dirt and working it to death.

This year I sowed the first seeds and onion sets at the end of March and tonight, on October 20, a killing frost will creep in from the desert and end the beautiful, charismatic work of my

JILLIAN LUKIWSKI

The edges of our land are brilliant with fall hues as the trees begin to give up their leaves. My garden has remained lush, colored with an array of flowers, ripe vegetables, and bushes of bright herbs. This has been the longest growing season of my life, a miraculously gentle Indian summer. I lift my face to a bluebird sky, I feel the wind and sun and energy of the day, and I give thanks.

bonafide green thumbs. The last of the fruit will fall from the orchard and those final glowing candies of summer will sweeten the Kunekune pigs we have grown to love and are raising to eat. The turkeys are cleaning up a mess of crab apples as they tartly fall from their branches; what a handsome thanksgiving feast our tom will make. The wind has battered the almond row and the plump green flesh that encloses an almond pit is an autumn treat the horses crave; they chew the flesh and spit out the pits like cowboys working on dips of tobacco. Chew, chew, chew and spit. While our livestock works to convert orchard fall into muscle and fat, our winter rye cover crop expands as a bright green fuzz across the garden vacancies. The growing season is over, but the farm continues to flourish as the death of the season is slowly consumed.

Yesterday, while at our backcountry elk camp, before the sun rose above the ten-thousand-foot peak to the east of our tent, and before the day had burned the frost off our golden meadow, I boiled water, brewed two cups of tea, and walked out of our tipi into the dim gray of morning. With two bulls down and one already packed out the ten miles to the trailhead, I felt we could take a moment to enjoy the break of day. I called my husband over and sat down with him on the ground beside the hot fence that held our grazing horses. I passed him a cup of tea and squeezed my body next to his to soak up some of his warmth. We sipped our drinks and placed all our faith in the arrival of a warm summer sun held hostage by a high-country rampart. The horses made their way toward us, bite by bite, and as they bit and ripped at the grass near our feet, I felt the ground reverberate beneath me. I felt the soil biome beneath us yanked up, pulled on, stretched out by horse teeth, and when the grass could finally bear no more, it broke, and I felt the earth snap back into place as my horses lifted their heads to chew their food with expressions of utter satisfaction. As they walked across their enclosure, I could see the meadow compress beneath their hooves, beneath the weight of their bodies, and then spring back into shape as they took another step.

As we watched our horses in the meadow, our hopes for our farm galvanized. We hope we might continue to build and maintain a dynamic farmscape on the solid back of soil that expands and contracts beneath our feet as we walk across it. We hope to foster and nurture a pliant biome that rolls with the punches and is made buoyant by vitality. We dream our homestead might mirror the resilience we see in the alpine meadows of elk country. We pray as we practice sovereignty over our food that the strength of the ecosystems we harvest our meals from echoes within us on a cellular level, making our bodies, minds, and souls supple and tenacious. We will boldly testify to the fact that we are what we eat.

NORTH STAR

JORDAN JONAS'S ART OF JOY & FREEDOM

Words by JACK EVANS *Photos by* ELIAS CARLSON

By the rendering of primetime television, Jordan Jonas is some master of loneliness. He was the winner of the sixth season of the History Channel show *Alone*. Painted as a contest of grit, skill and mental endurance, *Alone* drops thinly equipped contestants in separate reaches of the wilderness and awards $500,000 to the person who remains after all others have given up or been medically evacuated. Each season of the show spans months, and Jordan spent 77 cold days in his pole-and-branch shelter on the shores of Canada's Great Slave Lake to win Season Six.

When the show's crew picked him up, there was a part of Jordan that wasn't quite ready to leave.

His personal history carved him out well for the contest. Jordan had lived for cumulative years with Evenki reindeer herders in the middle of Siberia, simply for the joy of it. An Idaho farmboy by upbringing, he had hopped trains in his youth and worked around the country as a builder, usually raising money for returns to Russia. He fit the isolationist-hero's bill.

Within three weeks of initially being dropped in the Northwest Territories for the show, Jordan had hunted a moose with his recurve bow and immediately secured a winter's store of meat and fat. He was the first contestant in *Alone's* history to successfully kill a big game animal, but it didn't take long for wolverines to start raiding his supply. Jordan built an impressive Evenki-style cache in a day, but even this did not deter the thieves. He then rigged an alarm system out of tin cans, engineering a nighttime confrontation with the wolverine. He killed it in front of his shelter with a hatchet, which was probably the most intense thing ever seen on reality television.

Other contestants were valiantly subsisting on the dwindling returns of rabbit snares, and many were pulled from the contest after reaching life-threatening thresholds of starvation. Personal battles with isolation and despair were their stories.

Jordan, in the meantime, was settling in for the long haul.

"I expected it to go on at least twice as long as it did," Jordan said. "I kept thinking: 'I need to make it to 140 days, because somebody is going for the record.' Even when I got that moose, I thought: 'well somebody else has probably got a moose too.'"

While the competitive bushcraft element of *Alone* is exciting,

the show's real intrigue is the unfolding of personalities — some that thrive, some that suffer. Filmed by the contestants themselves, with tripods and body cams, *Alone's* pinnacle dramas are the inner monologues spilled out before the camera, the contestants' only conversation partner. Hunger, confusion, self-doubt and longing for family are common themes that arise as the days wear on. Persistence, stubbornness, and the slog toward the cash-prize goal tend to form the more aspiring side of contestants' dilemmas. What's fascinating, though, is that some people clearly struggle less, and their navigation of the endless, lonely campout casts them in a light of unbreakable, near-magic resolve.

Two months in, the remaining others were either desperately hungry or starting to make dangerous mistakes. By the time the Great Slave Lake froze over, Jordan was ice fishing with an Eskimo-style net-thread on homemade skis.

Because of all this, Jordan became a fascinating figure. While some competitors obsessed over the potential of the half-million dollars to transform their lives, Jordan mentioned it rarely. Nor did he seem to share in the psychological struggles of most of his rivals. It was like he had nothing to win and nothing to lose—and thus nothing to fear.

So, what was this magic recipe for fortitude?

I met him on a hazy summer afternoon in Idaho, to see what kind of personality he had – to meet this manic mountain man.

It took some work to find Jordan's home, down dusty roads in the hills north of Coeur d'Alene. He was raised on this farm. His mother owns it still, and there she was, working in their vegetable garden while two small grandchildren rolled around in its dirt.

Jordan appeared in a t-shirt and loose jeans, clearly coming from some work project. He greeted me with an enormous smile, welcoming me up to the house, where his wife Janahlee stood on the porch with a newborn baby. There were further introductions to make: to their two children, Ilana and Altai, five and three, and to Jordan's mother Ann.

We gathered around a rickety table on the old porch, and while I'd come with questions prepared, Jordan, at first had more for me. "How were the wildfires back in Montana? Are there many elk in my area? Do I have hunting plans this season?" We talked about fishing, kids, and a new perfection of handmade skis he's working on.

Jordan had just returned from hosting an immersive, weeks-long wilderness survival course in the mountains, and he was very happy to be home. In a few days, though, he was heading out into the Bitterroot Wilderness for a ten-day solo elk hunt.

"With a rifle?" I asked.

"Oh, no! Never. Well, once, with a muzzleloader. But I got started late in life, mainly in Russia." Since then, I've only hunted with a bow.

It was talk about hunting, and these deep immersions, that eventually led us to the topic of *Alone*.

"It was wonderful just being out there," Jordan said of his time in Canada. "Seeing the animals and thinking about them, even if you're not hunting them, you realize we're totally, not at all that different. And sometimes you could see the northern lights! And you're hearing the water freeze up, making these crazy sounds, with the insane light movement in the sky — it's just surreal."

"When it ended I couldn't believe it! I was ecstatic, but a little part of me was also thinking, 'Bummer. I didn't even feel like I was getting started yet.' It did seem too soon, in a way."

He hadn't had enough.

"But whatever that voice was, it was overshadowed by the shock and excitement. I was just thrilled to see my family again."

With Altai and Ilana clambering around him, I wondered how such a connected, familial person was able to stand the solitude — and why he would seek it out. Perhaps it was out of habit.

In 2006, Jordan, aged 22, received an invitation from an acquaintance to help build an orphanage with a missionary group in central Russia. He was living in Virginia at the time, and as he had throughout an ambitiously wild youth, he jumped at the chance for the journey.

"I went over there, but I didn't want to live with the American guys in the village because I wanted to learn Russian quicker. So they sent me to a neighboring village with these Russian families and I lived with them for a year. Two of the guys there had been in prison with an Evenki fellow and changed their lives, found God in prison and all that, so they kept saying to me: 'You've got to go meet our buddy up in the north!' Then one day he came through to sell furs and invited me to live with him. I spent a season with him and then he snowmobiled me out to his cousins, who were nomadic reindeer herders. He dropped me off at their tipi, vouched for me, and they took me in right away. I almost didn't know people like that existed until I met them."

Jordan returned to Siberia continually for over a decade and only missed his return this year because of travel restrictions. During that time, he spent cumulative years herding reindeer and went on his own months-long immersions, fur trapping and subsisting by himself. Such an adventure must have been hard to turn away from.

Throughout our conversation Jordan returned again and again to the theme of all that we've lost in our urbanized ways of life.

"You're not going to die from appendicitis here, and you're not going to starve if your hunt goes poorly. You have all these safety nets in the modern world, but you are never going to get the pure dopamine rush that you get like when I shot that moose, or when you catch one of those giant fish. I mean, when's the last time I literally jumped for joy like I did then? It's all-encompassing and it feels amazing to know that this gift, this animal, is meeting all your needs. We have such strange problems to navigate in this American way of life, but in Siberia they can still have it fairly purely."

The dilemma of 'two worlds' is common enough among adventurers. For some, the love of family and friends — of home — distracts from the drive forward, to discover, and the impulse to

search in the world alone. For others, the love of animals, extremity, and revelatory isolation — that freeing ground of the uninfluenced mind — draws them further and further away from human connection. I've known many people to struggle with reconciling these equal and worthy draws, so I asked Jordan if he had ever considered moving fully to the literal center of Siberia.

"Yeah," he said. "But the decision was hard. I kept thinking, 'I have a family back home, but I want to be included here in Russia.' I ended up pretty convinced that if my family was with me, and if Russian was my native tongue, I would choose that way of life over the modern way of life. We've gained so much in the modern world that I wouldn't want to give up, but we also don't really know what we've lost, you know? All these connections with our own creativity and resilience... it just feels like the way we're meant to be."

But for all his hermitic tendencies, Jordan kept recognizing his reliance on human connection, and with it, weighed the costs of a disappearance from his home world.

"When I first arrived in Siberia and was learning Russian, I remember thinking, 'I wouldn't wish this on my worst enemy.' I was mostly just laying in my bed, miserable. I think that was my starkest experience of isolation and it was pretty serious. Even though people are around, you're just missing all the jokes and the meaning, and in a weird way it was the harshest kind of lack of connection."

"But then you get through it and you learn those lessons. That really… prepared me."

Jordan learned how to herd reindeer and to ride them. He learned foraging and hunting, and, finally, became fluent in Russian.

He would return to America to renovate houses and earn money, always for the next Siberian immersion. All the while, he maintained a serious search for outer perspectives on the concept of resilience, to help him face battles with loneliness and the wild elements.

"I read *The Gulag Archipelago* in my early twenties, I think at the right time," he says, referring to Aleksandr Solzhenitsyn's epically painful and triumphant chronicle of Soviet prison camp survivors. "I thought a lot about what my grandparents went through."

Jordan's ancestors were ethnic Assyrians, hunted and persecuted en masse from modern-day Turkey to Armenia to Iran less than a hundred years ago. Jordan's grandmother and grandfather each saw nearly all of their family members killed, but managed to escape to America and raise a family "full of joy, and without hate."

"The Armenian Genocide was such a catastrophe, both for the culture and the individual," Jordan recounted. "My grandparents confronted all that real suffering in a way that maintained love and peace and hope. When I was young, I'd think: 'I'm pretty cold and lonely out here,' and then remember them. It puts a lot in perspective."

Across the span of his life, Jordan would recall what he knew of these ancestors in his most trying times.

"One of the Evenki guys was always talking about dreams. He would tell me about them, what he thought they meant, and ask me what I thought they meant. I usually have the dumbest, most pointless dreams in the world, so I never really understood him. But when I started trapping in Siberia all alone, my dreams all turned… vivid. They all became relevant. I was dreaming in ways that were speaking to my needs."

"I would go to sleep and be playing basketball with my brother, or something like that. I'd see family members, people I knew, and have these good and meaningful conversations — like they were with me. I started paying attention to their meanings, realizing that this was a tool, and it showed me how I was starved of human connection, and missed hanging out with the people I loved."

Jordan sought more of a balance, particularly after meeting his wife, Janahlee, and moving fully into a permanent home in America.

"A lot of my life I've been jumping between places," he told me. "For whatever reason, though, maybe it's experience or personality, I never get culture shock or this destabilization or anything. I'd be in Siberia, in the most remote place in the world, and then two days later be in New York City, hanging out with Janahlee and it'll seem pretty normal. The transition never bothered me, but I did miss the clarity and sense of being in the 'right place' that you can have when you're out there in the woods. It made me wonder if there were ways to integrate these two sides in some way. I don't know. It's interesting…" he trailed off.

Later on in life, at a friend's urging, he signed up as an applicant to *Alone*. He heard nothing, for years, until a History Channel casting director ultimately called him. He was added to Season Six's lineup, and while the show had visited British Columbia, Argentina and Mongolia in previous seasons, auspicious good fortune would have Jordan deployed to the Canadian Taiga.

"When I found out where we were going I was excited, because I know you can live by yourself there. That doesn't make it any easier to actually do, but the thought puts your survival in your own hands, at least, and you know you're not just being stuck out there for a starving contest."

Over the seasons, the "starving contest" mentality has become something of a motif on *Alone*. Each season, several contestants arrive with copious bushcrafting knowledge, but little experience living a protracted, settled hunter-gatherer lifestyle. Since no one had ever killed a large animal in five previous seasons, many contestants end up waiting on the days to pass, hoping to be crowned the winner before they grow too frail to remain in the bush.

Jordan, being the leanest — and probably the tallest — male contestant on Season Six knew that he would need a strategy to keep himself especially well-fed. He took on a whole different mentality.

"I was shocked that I was the only person to hunt a moose. The whole reason I had the confidence to sign up for the show is because I watched the first two seasons and nobody was hunting the bears! A lot of people were afraid of the bears. Some people, even a few who did very well, had never hunted before the contest. Weird time to start..."

Jordan himself had only started as an adult, in Siberia. Still, his eagerness for the pursuit showed — mistakes and all. Jordan stalked down the first moose that passed his camp and cleanly missed it.

"That was the biggest moose I had ever seen, and it was beautiful, awe-inspiring. I shot and missed and, funnily enough, I wasn't even disappointed. My thought was, 'This is like seeing a dinosaur. I have got to figure out a way to have another encounter.'"

He engineered another encounter using a technique not often seen in Canada — the "reindeer fence." By downing trees along well-worn animal paths, the Evenki are able to corral wild game and their own free-ranging, domestic reindeer. Jordan's fence perfectly redirected a second moose his way, and although he couldn't have known it, the successful hunt instantly upped the game of *Alone*.

Other contestants were struggling to garner rabbits. Jordan, taking another page from the Evenki lifeway, had set "at least a hundred and fifty snares," and kept busy in his free time by sewing a strikingly fashionable rabbit fur vest. *Alone* is designed, though, to simulate the truest sense of solipsism, and no contestant knows how their rivals are doing, nor how much longer they'll have to compete.

"By November, the lake had frozen over, and faster than I expected," Jordan said. "The moose and all the fish and rabbits made for plenty of meat, but I knew I'd need to get something big again to last the winter. I suppose I could have killed a musk ox if their migration came through towards spring… but I was thinking that by January everyone else would be so miserable, bored and cold that they'd quit. I knew that one of the most important things was to not let myself become bored."

The frozen shore of the Great Slave Lake, though, was Jordan's ideal playground.

"I'm not an artist in any way, but when you're in the woods, it's like your creative juices are flowing. You're thinking of all these things you can do to trick the animals, or to solve the issues that arise. It started making sense to me, how art developed, with people just coming up with these inventions out of their bright creativity. It's wonderful to be that tapped into it, whereas in the modern world, you can skim by so many problems without having to even process them. Out there, there's always problems and you're always having to come up with solutions. It seems like that same creativity develops into art and other things. Early humans, even when the living was rough, took the time to build figurines and carvings, and to paint. The source of that, which you can feel, is so interesting and so easy to lose track of in modern society."

Indeed, by the later days of Season Six, Jordan quite resembled a busy and curious early human. The living was rough, but he had not grown disenchanted in the slightest. He seemed to be integrating his entire life's interests into his winter campout on the

For some, the love of family and friends — of home — distracts from the drive forward, to discover, and the impulse to search in the world alone. For others, the love of animals, extremity and revelatory isolation — that freeing ground of the uninfluenced mind — draws them farther and farther away from human connection.

barren lakeshore. He seemed very happy.

Daily, he adjusted his food sources of moose meat, fishing net and rabbit traps. He perfected his cache system, but wolverines — genius thieves — found their way to his best, most nutritional stores of fat and organ meat.

"I kept thinking back to the books and to my grandparents' experience," Jordan said. "Having that perspective was invaluable. I think that made the suffering pretty easy. Facing constant problems, I tried to choose to proactively solve them, rather than stay in a reactive state all the time. I missed the first moose, so what can I do to make another encounter? The wolverine stole the meat, but what can I do to catch him next time?" It's more of a fight, rather than a flight mode."

Jordan got a fight. The wolverine prowled into his camp in the dark, tripping the wire-trap alarm. Jordan snuck out of his shelter to face the animal. He pinned it to the ground with one shot from a bow, and killed the wolverine while it hissed and snarled with a hatchet "A bit like this one," Jordan said, holding up a medieval-looking Evenki short-axe that was resting on the porch.

In his visceral victory over the wolverine, Jordan looked like the wildest of wildmen.

The second-to-last contestant dropped out of the show after two-and-a-half months on the ever-sharpening edge of hunger. *Alone's* safety crew then brought Janahlee with them to Jordan's snow-coated spruce hut.

She snuck up behind her husband and jumped into his arms by surprise. He was nearly knocked over. Jordan held her tight, could barely talk for his amazement, then apparently wanted nothing more than to show her around his spruce-branch home, his collection of smoked moose, and catch her up on the wolverine story.

"When I was younger," Jordan told me, "I was accumulating all these unique experiences, and I spent years out there doing all these really cool things. There came to be certain moments when it really struck me: all those things that were awesome or crazy or wild just stayed with me, and now my memory is going to forget it and it'll all be gone. Those experiences, even, are vain. That all turned into an interesting epiphany for me that my own, solo experience isn't the point of life."

"A lot of people complained about having the cameras out there, but I was infinitely grateful for it. In Siberia, I didn't have a camera. There were so many experiences that just went into my head and out the other side, and I can't explain them or relate them to people. Whereas on the show, all of a sudden, the people that I love were going to see this aspect of me! That goes beyond just telling a story."

"That was some of my motivation going out there. Even when I first talked to the History Channel, they asked me: "Why do you want to be on the show?" And I told them, "Well, what would I do to have a record like this from my grandpa?"

"It's cool to be able to deposit that into the world. The value of sharing is so important, and it made me not feel alone. Honestly, it's kind of abstract, but I just didn't really feel alone because the whole time I thought: 'I'm out here sharing this.'"

I knew that Jordan was appreciating sharing physical closeness with his family at the moment. His survival schools, now high in demand, keep him in the woods for a few months out of the year, and the elk hunting expedition he had planned for himself was days away. But before I left the farm, we decided to go for a wander in the nearby woods, and Altai and Ilana plodded along in tow.

The young brother and sister were equally talkative. As we walked, they narrated the path through the forest. "Sometimes we can catch a fish here," Altai told me. "I'm taking this branch," Ilana declared, dragging a pine bough larger than herself. "It's my bed."

Jordan seemed to have good partners for his life, lived between the wilderness and home. Indeed, over the course of the day, he had talked about an abstracted idea of bridging the gaps between the two by creating more nature-reliant, communal societies like the Evenkis'. He told me: "We lose track of what we miss out here in America. I've thought a lot about what it's like compared to Siberian life over the years, man. And I ask myself, 'what can we do?' And I think: 'maintain that here.'"

Here, walking into the woods with his family that was always with him, it seemed to me that Jordan was maintaining the love of life not in some wild, dreamlike, solipsistic path, nor in the sole safety of comfort, but in himself.

Words by LAILANI UPHAM *Photos by* LOUISE JOHNS

LAILANI UPHAM — LOUISE JOHNS

THE BUFFALO STONE

The relationship between Native Americans and buffalo has survived days of plenty and days of tragedy. Now, as bison resurgence efforts gain traction across a number of tribes and government institutions, Modern Huntsman turns its attention to the milieu of interests, perspectives and histories that inform the fraught and complex conservation of the bison.

In this installment of our continued coverage, Lailani Upham writes from the Blackfeet Reservation in Montana, following the threads of her peoples' stories back several millennia to the beginning of the human-bison encounter as we know it. Photographer Louise Johns accompanies, documenting a present-day reinvigoration of Blackfeet culture that's come on the back of a growing tribal buffalo herd.

Native peoples' freedom to hunt, manage and care for buffalo is still on its way back from the brink — the harshest days of settler colonization, experienced in the 19th and 20th centuries. Still, new initiatives to reintroduce bison herds to tribal lands are slowly succeeding. As they progress, bringing hope and greater means of self-determination to Native America, Modern Huntsman will be reporting. The American relationship with bison is as emblematic of the West's violent past as it is of the human capacity to protect, revere, and recognise interdependence with great beings outside of ourselves. Many voices must be heard in the search for a better socio-ecological future. Here, we visit some of the longest-standing stories on the landscape: those of the Blackfeet Tribe.

LAILANI UPHAM — LOUISE JOHNS

BLACKFEET RESERVATION, MT

Everything in the Blackfoot peoples' existence begins with a story. If you spend any time on the Blackfeet reservation in Montana or any of the Blackfoot Confederacy reserves in Canada, you will hear that every living creature on the earth, in the sky and and in the water is connected through a saga and through a ceremony.

There's a story that was told to me by my great uncle and the Chief of the Blackfeet Nation, Earl Old Person. It is a story of our connection to buffalo.

Earl, 91, one of the oldest living elders of the Amskapi Pikunii (one of four bands of the Blackfoot Confederacy), kept his fluency in the old language throughout his century. The real Blackfoot language carries spirit and meaning that is lost in translation to the English language which is sadly the current language of our people due to U.S. government intrusion. But that's another story for another day.

When you're in the presence of Chief Earl, you're able to surrender present-day existence and enter the days of bygone ancestors. Earl's soothing, melodic and thoughtful speech touches the spirit of a person; the sharing of a Blackfoot oral story is a full, felt, sweeping experience.

"The buffalo was our way of life," he says. "It was everything to us. But there was a time way back when our people could not hunt the buffalo." Earl says the time of this ancient story took place during a wicked winter. He describes a lake and a high ridge called Where the Cherries Were Smashed, located on present-day Blackfeet Reservation lands in Montana. "We have a place over here called Buffalo Lake. It is where a lot of buffalo roamed in the winter time," he continues, motioning in Indian sign language. "But this time they weren't there. The people were getting hungry, and they were going all over trying to find the buffalo. One woman went looking for buffalo on her own and while walking, she heard a song. She checked to see if anyone was around and could see no one. Every time she walked she heard the song. She forgot about the buffalo and started looking for this song. Where is it coming from? As she got closer she noticed the sound was coming from the ground. Finally, she came up on a stone, a buffalo stone. The stone was telling her where to find the buffalo." And Earl begins to sing the song.*

> THOSE BLACK ANIMALS WITH LONG BEARDS WERE ARMED; AND ONCE, AS THE PEOPLE WERE MOVING ABOUT, THE BUFFALO SAW THEM, AND HOOKED THEM, AND KILLED AND ATE THEM. THE CREATOR WAS TRAVELLING OVER THE COUNTRY AND SAW ONE OF HIS CHILDREN EATEN BY A BUFFALO. HE BECAME VERY SAD. HE SAID, 'THIS WILL NOT DO. I WILL CHANGE THIS. THE PEOPLE WILL EAT THE BUFFALO.'
>
> —
>
> GEORGE BIRD GRINELL, *Blackfoot Tales*

"This is the song; we use it today. Ervin Carlson has a buffalo restoration program and they use it. They call it I-nis'-kim — Buffalo Stone. And this is the one stone and song that gave the people direction."

"If we don't have a story of something that exists now, then it just isn't so," says Darnelle Rides At The Door, a Pikunii elder, a knowledge keeper, and one of our traditional leaders. "That's the way most Native people are." She says the traditional stories bring us back to the original understanding of what makes us Blackfoot. "If we can go back and remember our story, as a people of the plants and animals, through our 'Napi stories' that explain our existence with other living creatures, then we can honor other living things — on and below the Earth." Napi stories are the Blackfoot creation stories and draw pictures of how and why nature does what it does, she explains. "So the how and why of things are really important for us." Through the stories and songs, our identity to the natural world is understood not only through our mindful understanding, but more importantly through our spiritual reality and position as Niitsitapi (people).

The Iinnii, or buffalo, is a representative of our way of life and a representative of our environment, and the way things came about in our environment. "Way back in ancient times, buffalo ate people, and that's a Napi story itself," Darnelle reminds me. It is the story of the Blackfoot genesis. Part of it tells of a day when the Iinnii dominated the plains. An excerpt from the English-language record, the 1892 book Blackfoot Tales by ethnologist, writer and Blackfeet nation friend George Bird Grinnell, reads: "Those black animals with long beards were armed; and once, as the people were moving about, the buffalo saw them, and hooked them, and killed and ate them. The Creator was travelling over the country and saw one of his children eaten by a buffalo. He became very sad. He said, 'This will not do. I will change this. The people will eat the buffalo.'" The story continues with divine direction on how to hunt and use all parts of the animal in an honorable and prayerful way. The Creator went on to tell the people the Iinnii will come to them in dreams, prayers and ceremonies to guide them.

"The Creator showed us how to prepare the meat from head to toe with nothing wasted," Darnelle said. "The hides went to lodges, clothing and heavy blankets. The fur and hair was made into ropes; the buffalo hooves are used in ceremonies and bring a unique sound that honors the Iinnii, paired with a song. This is a calling bringing the buffalo back." The Iinnii has so much to offer in the life of the people, she explained. The Iinnii cultivate the environment through other animals and plants. "The Iinnii is a planter of seeds. When a little buffalo bird lands on a buffalo, it is there for a reason," says Darnell. She says the bird puts seeds in the fur, and when the buffalo shakes around its head, it spreads the seeds to the ground. The buffalo then digs its hooves in the ground to create a culvert for the seeds to grow.

During the 19th century, Iinnii were hunted nearly to extinction by American settlers. A combination of horrific U.S. policy, non-Native land-grabs, and settler encroachment took a vast toll on the main source of sustenance for the Blackfeet. Millions of buffalo were killed, along with hundreds of thousands of Native Americans across the land. By the turn of the century, less than a hundred Iinnii remained. Buffalo were hunted for their fur and tongues, while the rest of the animal was abandoned to decay. After the animals rotted, their bones were collected and shipped back east in large quantities. It was known to the plains tribes who relied on the bison that the slaughter was a policy from the U.S. government to starve Native Americans into submission.

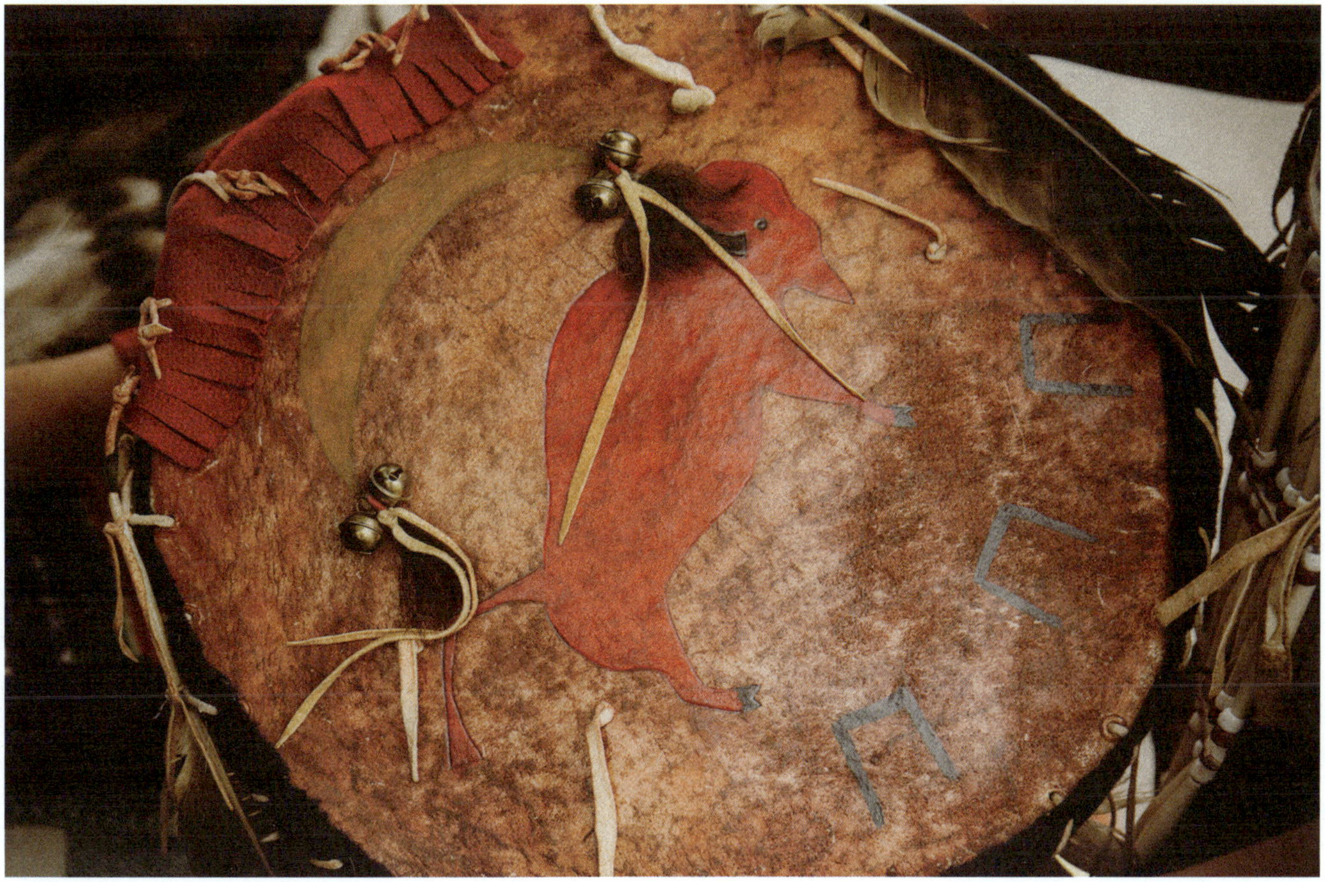

LAILANI UPHAM — LOUISE JOHNS

Unlike the Indigenous, tribal people who killed for food, clothing and shelter, the hunters from the East killed mostly for destruction. The Blackfoot and other plains tribes looked on with traumatized dismay as landscapes and prairies were littered with rotting buffalo carcasses. The kills were a result of advertised excursions for "hunting by rail." Trains encountered massive herds alongside or crossing tracks, and the men aboard climbed to the roofs, took aim, and left countless 1,500-pound animals dead to rot.

Blackfeet Tribal Buffalo Program Director Ervin Carlson said the Iinnii began to trickle back onto the Blackfeet reservation in 1974. The first season of return encountered little support from outsiders, as well as some disinterest from within the Blackfeet community. "They weren't used to this wild animal anymore because they had been gone for so long," he said. Carlson, a Native cattle rancher, explains that at the time, he didn't totally understand or feel the connection. "I really didn't care one way or another until they (the bison) were put under my care." Carlson was hired on as the tribal Agriculture Manager in 1996 and shortly afterward was asked to take over the management of the bison. From the start, it has been a challenging, yet rewarding, learning, growing and even healing journey for him.

"You'd like to think the discrimination and racism is not there and we are past those things," says Carlson. But in many non-Native ranchers it persists, which Ervin realized after working with tribal buffalo projects in efforts to bring them back. "In my early years, when I was president of the InterTribal Buffalo Council, we received the 2005 Conservation Achievement Award from the National Wildlife Federation for 'extraordinary contribution to the conservation of wildlife and natural resources'." Carlson recalls attending a large conference of congressional representatives in Washington, D.C., where he spoke on behalf of the council receiving the award. He said he spoke from the heart rather than relying on a prepared speech. Carlson presented a rundown on what the Blackfeet Buffalo program was doing to restore the bison to the traditional homeland. Carlson spoke of the hurdles he witnessed firsthand around the state of Montana. "I told them that the buffalo were almost killed to extinction and the reason was, they thought if you get rid of the buffalo that's when you are going to get rid of the Indian. I said that the buffalo are still here and we are bringing the buffalo back — and we're still here." He remembers this statement receiving a loud applause; he had expected a different response.

The Iinnii that many believed were lost in history are once again grazing on Blackfeet territory. The I-nis'-kim story is a modern-day prophecy of the Blackfoot Confederacy.

"Hunting is a ceremony, not a sport," said Terraine Edmo, or Awanaaki (Rattle Woman), the Blackfeet Climate Change Coordinator. She explained that Iinnii always protected the people. "In a sense the buffalo is like our leader, and guides us in our way of life," she said. "We [both Indians and buffalo] have had to fight all our lives."

"Blackfeet people are connected to the animals," says Joe Wagner, 34, a member of the Crazy Dogs Society of tribal leaders. Wagner said when hunting is done as a sport, it removes the spiritual engagement of the people with both their animal relatives and their past. "We are disconnecting our identity and stunting our spiritual growth."

Blackfoot people know their connection to the sacred four-legged relative to be powerful. "We learned to follow them as patterns in life. Look at the power they have to face a storm," says Wagner. "Just as the buffalo face and walk toward a storm and know there is light on the other side; they have taught us not to turn away from our problems."

Edmo says the tie Blackfeet have with the Iinnii is a common thread. "We're not going anywhere; we are going to continue our being and tradition until the last."

To hear the I-nis'-kim song, and to read more from this series visit* ***modernhuntsman.com*

LAILANI UPHAM — LOUISE JOHNS

THE
RUGG
IS
EAL

HUNTSMAN

AN INTERVIEW SERIES

From the beginning, Modern Huntsman has strove to be a bipartisan forum, and bring in diverse perspectives from often opposing viewpoints, in hopes of having constructive conversations where they are otherwise not being had. Whether it's debating the nuances of hunting ethics, dietary choices, or especially politics, we feel that the future of hunting depends on our collective ability to broaden the range of people in these conversations, and find common ground. To seek the greater good, expand horizons, and be empathetic towards those who might think, act, or live differently than us, rather than continue the destructive cycle of divisiveness that has turned so many away from this community over the years. It is our intention with this new interview series to continue that mission, to pull the curtain back for those willing, and cultivate an open space to have real conversations. Which leads to our first interview.

NFL athlete, celebrity, and somewhat of an enigmatic, controversial figure, Jay Cutler is no stranger to being in the spotlight, or in the hot seat for that matter. Quarterbacking for the Denver Broncos and Chicago Bears for nearly a decade, he faced public criticism for a seemingly cavalier and brazen attitude. His personal life is often in the headlines, leading to a lot of speculation about the type of person that Jay is, though very few detractors likely know, and even fewer asked what he thinks. As Jay embarks on a new chapter in life, he wants to step up to the mic. So during the final days of archery season in Montana, I hosted Mr. Cutler at my house to address some of these things. We hunted elk in a snowstorm, cooked great food, drank more than a few beers, and covered a wide range of conversational topics. It's not often that you get to see the real side of someone you've watched on TV, but it was an honor getting to hear more about Jay's interests, philosophy and visions for life after football. It's clear that he has more to say than he's been able to thus far. We talked about criticism in the public eye, overcoming adversity, and the struggles that come with leadership. But mostly we talked about where he wants to go now, and where his true passions lie. Intelligent, quick-witted, and diverse, Jay represents a glimpse into mainstream crossover culture, which qualifies him as a candidate for this new interview series, Huntsman at Large.

Interview & Photos by TYLER SHARP

AT LARGE

A conversation with

JAY CUTLER

TYLER SHARP

Many folks know you from your NFL career, appearances on TV, or sensationalized headlines, but most people probably don't know about your passion for hunting. Tell us about your upbringing. How were you introduced to it?

JAY CUTLER

It started with my dad. We were raised lower middle class in Indiana, and hunting was a way for him to bring meat to the table. Every single dollar was either going toward the family, the kids, or some way to make our lives better. He could subsidize meat that way, and that's how it all started. I just remember my mom saying, "We need to get a deer this year. We need something in the freezer." It's evolved from that point, but it was a means to an end. We needed that protein and that food. I started going out with him more, and I remember the first time that I actually shot at a deer, a doe. I think I was probably nine or ten. My dad took two-by-fours and built almost a tree house. We're sitting in this damn thing, in the snow, and it was freezing out there. Deer hunting, for a kid, can be really tough sometimes. If you're not seeing a lot, it's cold; it's just hard. I took my first shot with a 20-gauge 870 Remington shotgun. I hit low, and we never found her. It really affected me negatively, and from that point on, I didn't really hunt that much. I was playing sports, doing a million other things, and it just took a back-burner.

TYLER

When did you re-discover it?

JAY

Growing up, I just wasn't really allowed inside that much, I was always outside playing. It was always in me, and there has always been a draw to the outdoors, and something I find being out there: peace and tranquility. After that first doe mishap, it just wasn't my main focus — sports was. It wasn't until later in my career, when I was about 30, and we were starting to have kids, that it came full circle. I was looking at the quality of food and meat in the U.S. at that time, and our family was really getting into organics, non-GMOs, and all that stuff. It took me back and I thought, *Oh, I remember*. That's why we first started hunting. That got the engines pumping again and I realized how much I'd missed that part of my life.

TYLER

During demanding times in your career, how has hunting served you? What does it mean to you?

JAY

Playing sports is a performance, it's entertainment. That's what you're doing. From the time that I was eight or nine, I feel like I've been putting on a show. To have found this other passion in hunting, something that brings me peace and allows me to get away from stress, has been great. The more that I get back into it, the more joy I find in it, especially in the past three or four years. To me, it's not really about just going out there to harvest an animal, or even just to find peace. Now it's more about enjoying different interests in my life, things that took a backseat for so long. I never really had a backup plan. It was never, "If football doesn't work out, I'm going to do X, Y and Z." That never crossed my mind. I was committed to, and 100 percent involved in that, for 20 years.

TYLER

I know that hunting can have a healing effect, but with all of the public scrutiny in the media, is that a part of your life that you've tried to keep quiet?

JAY

No, I didn't keep it quiet. Personally, I just felt that I wanted to have something that was private, that was mine. Playing football comes with a lens into every part of your life. On the field, off the field, you're being watched and scrutinized. I did a reality show with who I was married to at the time, and there were many aspects of my life that were very open, and were very public. That was part of the job, and I understand that. I just wanted to have something that was mine, that I could live in, have fun with, and breathe a little bit.

TYLER *This issue is themed around resilience, and that's definitely a word that you must've relied on during your career. What does that word mean to you?*

JAY Resilience? To me, it's vital. Not everyone has it, and not everyone goes through the same trials and tribulations. There's a lot of people that would look at my life, and say, "He has everything he could ever want. Why is resilience even a part of his vocabulary?" From my perspective, I feel like I've been through a lot. I've overcome a lot, but I'm sure not everyone can see that, because I don't talk about it much. I think that's what the outdoors, and hunting, and that whole world has given me — an escape from those types of things, and a chance to reset.

TYLER *You were faced with a lot of criticism in the NFL. Your character was attacked, and often painted in a negative light. You were someone people loved to hate, because you didn't really fit the mold for a typical NFL quarterback. How did you navigate those detractors or public slanders and stay focused on your goals and your happiness?*

JAY You know, I've ignored it for so long, because I didn't want to bring that energy into my life. I was concentrated on football, and it just felt like it was a distraction. I never wanted to be famous. I wanted no part of that. I don't like the attention. Early in my career, social media wasn't a thing. You could kind of hide, especially in Denver. But going to Chicago, all the social media like Twitter and the press just made the world a much smaller place. Being in that spotlight, everyone wants a lot of you. They want to know who you are, and know everything about you. They're going to cut down certain things, and attack your character. There's just nowhere to hide. Being out of football, and being in a different phase of my life, I find myself wanting to face those criticisms, and show a completely different side than when I was on the football field, or what people may have read in dramatized headlines. Being an NFL quarterback for 12 years, and trying to lead a group of guys on offense, I think you have to have a little bit of a stoic personality. You've got to be able to let those things go, because you're going to hear them regardless. But for me, I just felt that for the other 10 guys out there, I had to try to be above all that. I just ignored it all, and let that rhetoric go. Whether it was true or not, I didn't really respond much at all. Now, as I'm getting older, I find that some of those stigmas bother me, because they aren't true, and they're not who I am. Going forward, these are things that I want to face. I want to show different aspects of my personality, and different interests that I have. Because for whatever reason, I think I'm going to have a platform to do that.

TYLER *We've received a lot of criticism for trying to do something different, and affect long-term change in terms of inclusivity and diversity. There is a toxic mentality that prevails, where if you are not part of "the club," then you are chastised, and I think it has a lot to do with the reason why the hunting industry is shrinking. What are your thoughts on the divisiveness within the industry, and how do you see a path forward?*

JAY Honestly, I think it's the best thing you have on your side. I think the traditional hunting world is dated, and that's part of why we're losing so many hunters every year. There's a million other things to do in the world right now: camping, fishing, hiking, climbing, or just being out in nature. I think COVID, and everything that's happening has pushed people in that direction. I think there's a chance to take that momentum, and build on it. But to me, it's not going to be done by the old-school hunting types. It's just not. It's going to be done by Modern Huntsman, yourself, and everyone that's involved. Folks that are a little bit more worldly, have different interests, who are into food, travel, and even fashion and clothing. To me, that's what the future of hunting looks like.

I know you have interest in culture and style, but those are words that aren't usually related to a lot of things in the hunting and outdoor industries. Where do you see room for those things to be brought in, and create an environment that improves the culture around hunting, and makes it a little more approachable? **TYLER**

I think approachable is the word. It's daunting for someone that is interested in hunting, but maybe they're a CPA in Chicago, and they just don't know the first thing about actually doing it. They want to go out there and harvest something, but they're stuck in a city. Personally, I want to help bridge the gap for them, and be a conduit that says, "You know what? I love being in cities too. I love New York. I love Dallas. I love Chicago. I love going to these cities, eating the food, going shopping, and seeing the fashion. But I also like to hunt. There's also a side of me that loves being in Montana." I don't think you have to pick one or the other. You just don't. I think you can do both really well, and at a high level. **JAY**

Apart from helping bridge that gap, you were diagnosed with Type 1 diabetes, which is rare for professional athletes. It was late onset, right? **TYLER**

Yes. I think it was 10 years ago now. It was my second year playing in the NFL, I was in Denver, and I lost 30 pounds throughout the season. The last game, I played at 202 pounds, or something crazy. We were playing the Vikings, and a couple guys from their team came over and asked, "What is wrong with you, man?" I honestly had no idea. **JAY**

I know that being an athlete, there's an emphasis on performance, fitness and eating healthy, especially with the added complexity of diabetes, but how does that all cross over? What's the importance of it to you now? **TYLER**

It's obviously really important in my life, because it's something I think about, literally every single day with Type 1 diabetes. When we started having kids, we went down the rabbit hole of processed foods, white flour, and white sugar. How that affects your glucose, and your sugar. Protein is one of those things that's overlooked. I think we're in a huge gluten phase, carb phase, sugar phase. But some of the proteins, they're injected with all kinds of stuff. Not everyone is capable, I realize that, but hunting is a way to bring home healthy meat for your family. That is either often overlooked, or too daunting of an experience for people to try to undertake. Going forward, it's something that I think is important, to find a way to make that more accessible to everybody. **JAY**

Tell us a little bit more about your love of food, and where hunting overlaps. Do you value your time in the kitchen? **TYLER**

I love food, and I love going to restaurants and tasting new stuff. I love the artistic nature of it, because it is absolutely an art form. It blows my mind to see some of the things that chefs create. But I really love trying to take some of those recipes, and trying to put some of the wild game I've harvested into it: elk, turkey, pheasants, whitetail, whatever it is. The health benefits are really important to me, especially with my diabetes, and I want my kids to grow up as healthy as they possibly can. We didn't eat great growing up, and that's not on my parents, we just didn't know, the science wasn't there. They were doing the best they possibly could, and I don't blame them at all. But we're just so much more knowledgeable now, and for me as a parent, it would be a crime not to try to do that for my kids. I've got two sons and a daughter, and I love to cook for them. I think it's really important for my boys, and my daughter, to understand that the kitchen space isn't just for women. That's not the case at all. I can get in there, and mix it up, and I definitely want my boys to know how to cook, and be able to take care of themselves. If they have a family someday, I want them to be able to step into that role, because that's the future. Women aren't going to take a backseat anymore, nor should they. They should be chasing **JAY**

down and doing whatever they want to do. I think relationships in general are going to have to be much more equally weighted, in all aspects.

TYLER *You talked about helping bridge the gap for hunting with the mainstream public. In your opinion, where do you feel like that disconnect is between the natural food sourcing you're talking about, and the negative connotations people make when they hear the word hunting?*

JAY I think it's just a lack of knowledge. I think it's going to take groups like Modern Huntsman to bridge that gap. I was just talking to somebody today about how over in Europe, many hunters dress in green and brown tweeds, and I asked them, "What do you think about hunters over there?" They said, "Well, I think they're really classy." That can be done here in the U.S. as well, so that less people think we're just a bunch of rednecks out there, firing off rounds. I think you have to portray it in a different way. Which, apart from you guys, just hasn't really been done much. That doesn't take away from anything that anyone's done in the past, or what they're doing right now, but I think the focus should be less on the current hunters, and more on how we recruit new people to this lifestyle. I think there's so many aspects that could help better their lives: being outdoors, getting lean protein, being in touch with nature, putting phones down. I think there's a huge array of positives that can come from it.

TYLER *We're launching this new series, Huntsman At Large, to highlight a diverse range of folks who have hunting as one of many aspects of their life. What does that term mean to you, and what sort of people do you feel like would be interesting to feature?*

JAY Well, I think we've touched on it briefly through this. I think "At Large" are the key words there. I don't want to be labeled as just a hunter. I love hunting, and I would never shy away from that by any means, but there's so many more aspects to my life, and my interests. But like we talked about, the food part. The travel part. The outdoors part. The camping. The fashion part. Sports. There's a litany of things that make up who I am, and hunting just happens to be one that I have a huge passion for, but I don't want to just be limited to that role. I think going forward, you're going to find some amazingly talented people that undercover hunt and don't tell anybody about it. Maybe they're an artist in New York, and they're going upstate or to Maine or something, and shooting stuff. I think that's going to open up some doors for people to express their love for hunting, and show other interesting aspects of their lives. But to accomplish this, you have to show people. They have to see it. Everyone can read stuff, but I think going forward, you have to provide examples: "All right. We're interested in this. We're doing this other thing. We're part of this world. Hunting is also a part of our life, and it's not a bad thing, it's just something else that we do." It can't be just about hunting, because it needs to appeal to more people. The bigger your range, the bigger the audience is going to become. But you will also face much bigger challenges.

TYLER *I knew when we started that it was going to be a difficult journey, and it has been. But it's also been very rewarding, and that keeps us marching onward. In the spirit of resilience and pushing ahead, what would your advice be for somebody reading this who might be going through some challenging times?*

JAY It's hard. It's really hard, but I think that's also life. I'm sure there's a handful of people out there that never really had a lot of tribulations, but I think 99.9 % of people have some sort of hardship. That's part of it. I'm currently going through one now. If you don't learn anything from it, I think you're missing the boat. You have to learn from it. You have to grow from it, or it's going to happen again sometime later in life. It just is. You have to take your responsibility: "Why am I here? What did I do to get myself in this mess?" You make 1,000 choices every day. Sometimes they're right, and sometimes they're the wrong ones, and they lead to something that hurts, or puts you in a bad spot. But you

THERE'S DEFINITELY GOING TO BE TIMES WHERE YOU'RE JUST BLESSED AND SOMETHING FALLS IN YOUR LAP, BUT THE MAJORITY OF TIMES, IT'S GOING TO BE A BATTLE.

can learn from those and say, "I would do this differently. I wouldn't do this differently. I learned patience, or some other virtue." But you can figure out your own mindset, and make choices that are going to put you in the best position possible. If you can do that, and keep moving forward, you're going to be better off.

TYLER

We were dealt a pretty heavy deck of obstacles this year, and I've been working on trying to remove myself from making that a personal thing. Obstacles or challenges don't care about you individually, and they're going to keep coming. All you can control is the way you react to them, and focus on what you have to do to persevere.

JAY

For sure. There is going to be another one around the corner. Nothing's going to go smoothly all the time. There's definitely going to be times where you're just blessed and something falls in your lap, but the majority of times, it's going to be a battle. Especially whenever you're trying to do something that's against norms, or there's a backlash, or people that disagree with you. You've just got to follow your heart.

TYLER *If you had an event, that would represent the achievement or progress toward that goal, who are some of the types of people that you'd want to be in that room, having that conversation?*

JAY I think you would take a mom of four. I think you would take some sort of impressionist artist that works in a studio. I think you'd take a Wall Street banker. I think you'd take someone from the South, that has grown up killing hogs all the time. I think you'd take someone from California or Oregon, or something like that, who despises guns. I think you can make a mixing pot of all these different people. Maybe they don't hunt. Maybe they see it differently. I think if you can start accomplishing that, then you're on the right track.

TYLER *For those people that maybe aren't hunters, what do you say to them to get their interest piqued, or gain their respect?*

JAY I think actions speak a lot. Doing things the right way, and showing them through various media, is going to be huge. Having an open mind as a hunter and listening to what they want to say. How they want to say it. What their concerns are. That's also important. You get into a certain stigma as a hunter, of saying, "What we're doing is right. You're not taking away our guns. We're going out there. We're doing this. We're doing that." That's not going to work. You have to have some sort of middle ground, and have empathy for both sides. Because I don't think I can tell them anything, and I'm not going to convince them of going against the grain. I'm not trying to do that. I just want to have an understanding. "I'll understand your side. I need you to understand my side. Watch my actions. See how I do this." You can take that any way you want, but that doesn't even have to be hunting. It can be the farthest thing from hunting. It could be that you know where to find wild mushrooms. It could be being vegan. I think that's the narrative. That's the direction of where this thing has to go. You have to educate people. You have to show them what you're about.

TYLER *I think, if anything, ethical hunting is part of that natural order. Sure, the tools and the technology have changed a little bit. But more so, making sure that there's an understanding. Even with somebody who maybe is vegan or vegetarian, they're going out to forage, making sure that they at least have an understanding of the natural cycle. Hunting plays a role in that, regardless of what their dietary choices are.*

JAY I think that's why it's important to focus on the word "modern." Because it's not the 1980s. It's almost 2021. The world has changed. People have changed. I think that the more the dialogue heads in that direction, the more people are going to take notice, and think, *Okay. They're talking about this in a different way.* Which I think is the starting point. Then you have to show them a different way. I think it's an exciting time for Modern Huntsman. You guys are on the forefront of a lot of change. Going forward, your company and the people you have on your team are going to help lead that charge. It's going to be a wild ride, but I think it's going to be a lot of fun to watch.

TYLER *You've accomplished a lot, and now being retired from football you can pretty much go any direction you want in this new chapter. Fast forward 20 years — what do you want your legacy to be?*

JAY That's a great question. Like I said earlier, I've played football and sports for so long. That was it. That was Plan A. There was no Plan B. The past year has given me an opportunity to think about where my passions are, and what I really love. Football obviously was one, and replacing that is going to be really, really hard because I started at such a young age, and I did it for so long. But now I'm thinking about what I really liked doing as a kid. What gave me a sense of freedom? What did I wake up in the morning, and think, *I'm excited to go do this.* Some of the hunts that I've been able to experience the past few years have brought me to the conclusion that it's something that I want to do in the future. I just don't want to do it the same way it's been done the last 20 years. I want to be on the forefront of how we change the culture and mindset of hunting. How do we get some people that you never would have thought wanted to hunt into this world? I would also like to address current hunters and talk more about other aspects to life. How do we change the whole mindset? The whole organization?

TYLER

It's interesting. A lot of hunters face challenges with how they're perceived, and they don't know how to talk about it. They don't know how to share the fact that maybe they're into Dungeons and Dragons. Maybe they're into Lady Gaga. Whatever it is. In that regard, it's important to find ways to give people comfort and confidence to diversify.

JAY

It's huge. I think you have to be open about who you are. I don't care how big of a hunter you are. It doesn't matter to me. You could be the most hardcore western ram or goat hunter in the world, but you're also doing other stuff. You just are. You've got a job. You've got hobbies. You've got kids. You've got something else going on in your life. It's just a fact. Wrapping yourself in the hunting world, and saying, "I'm a hardcore hunter. I have to just hunt, hunt, hunt, hunt" — it's not realistic, or real. I would rather be with people who are more practical and be able to say, "Yeah, I definitely enjoy hunting. But I'm going to be in New York in two weeks, and I'm going to be in the meatpacking district, walking around in whatever I'm wearing. It's not going to be hunting clothes, I can tell you that." That's part of my life. I think that we just have to open up to that reality here, really soon.

TYLER

It's an interesting opportunity for you. Where previously you weren't very vocal, now you have this platform with a lot of people listening and watching, and have the chance to take the mic. Whether you like it or not, you are influential to a lot of people, and have the opportunity to take what you have learned and share that with a larger audience, and be an inspiration.

JAY

For sure. That's exactly what I want to do. I want to help bridge the gap between the current hunters that live in this bubble, and the rest of the world — people that might look down on hunting, or are scared to get into it. Whatever it is, I'm ready for that role. Going back to the word resilience, and overcoming things; what I did, going through all the media, the scrutiny, has given me the ability to face those challenges. I don't know if confidence is the word, but it's not daunting. It doesn't bother me. That history of what I've done is going to serve me well going forward.

THAT HISTORY OF WHAT I'VE DONE IS GOING TO SERVE ME WELL GOING FORWARD.

TYLER SHARP & JAY CUTLER

SELLING THE DREAM

Story by DJ STRUNTZ

Kimi Werner is a professional hunter. She doesn't fit the stereotypical mold of a rough-hewn African safari guide. Instead, this soft-spoken, flip-flop-wearing island girl from Maui holds her breath and wears a neoprene wetsuit to work. Her capabilities should not be underestimated, nor her ready smile mistaken for weakness. She is a consummate professional; an absolutely lethal underwater hunter. A former U.S. National Spearfishing Champion, Kimi is perhaps the most widely respected and recognized female diver in the sport. Her phone never stops ringing. Chase snappers in Mexico, wahoo in Texas, tunas in Ascension — the options are endless, as are the expectations. Jetting from one location to the next becomes a blur of perpetual motion. Perceptions must be maintained, decisions defended, obligations met, and above all, content created. The tension of meeting the constraints of her contractual obligations to her sponsors is the accepted cost of the freedom she enjoys — the freedom offered by an escape into the depths of the ocean she so dearly loves. These worlds collided on a trip to the Azores, an often-overlooked island chain to which she felt inexplicably linked.

The Azores might best be described as the love child of Portugal and Hawaii. The weather-worn cobblestone streets in its towns are lined with bustling cafes that scream Europe, juxtaposed against lush green countryside adorned with exotic plants like ginger and taro that spirit you away to Kona or Kauai. It is a beautiful fusion of old-world tradition and island exuberance.

Landing on the tiny volcanic island of Pico, she stepped off our plane, into the syrupy autumn afternoon sunshine and searched for her local host. The man meeting her *was* Azorean spearfishing. Kimi had heard rumbles about Paulo Afonso in her world, murmurs about a diver who most often dove alone and returned to shore with massive tunas that defied believability. Scouring his social media only confirmed her suspicions. This guy was a human shark — he lived to battle sea monsters, and she had come to do the same.

The blaring klaxon of the alarm the following morning was both unwelcome and excitedly anticipated. As we chugged inky black, home-brewed espresso, spear guns, gear bags, and my underwater camera rigs

were hurriedly loaded into the Pearla Negra — Paulo's seven-meter rigid-hull inflatable boat. The rumble of the four-stroke motor shattered the quiet of the predawn darkness as we left the shelter of the tiny harbor and headed out into the open expanse of the Atlantic. For the next five exhausting days, the routine never wavered. Rise in the dark, load the boat, run to a spot, dive, dive, dive, and head to the next spot. Repeat ad nauseam until dark. Return to the harbor, scarf food, crash.

Pinnacle after pinnacle, reef after reef, bait ball after bait ball, searching for quarry to no avail. Kimi proceeded with a brave face, pushing her diving to its limits to get fish. Paulo kept apologizing for his island's indifference. The strain was taking a toll. Conversations focused solely on the task at hand. Exhaustion, both physical and mental, was apparent. The big game fish simply were not cooperating or had seemingly relocated to another ocean entirely. They were failing, and pushing harder wasn't yielding different results. Emotions often masked by the elation of success began to percolate to the surface.

Night five, after a seemingly never-ending day of oxygen-deprived narcosis, we decided to indulge in the obvious offering: food and an excess of wine. Empty bottles began to accumulate beneath the crazy starlit sky as Paulo and Kimi discussed their options.

"Fishing is just hard here — I'm always concerned about inviting anyone, because you can never predict if the fish will really be here or not," Paulo explained. Kimi, lost in her own thoughts, barely acknowledged his comment. She was somewhere else.

On impulse, Kimi told Paulo:

DJ STRUNTZ

"My best friend had always wanted to come here. She always talked about the Azores when we travelled together."

Paulo asked, "Where is she?"

"She died six years ago."

Kimi started crying. There was a weight of emotion, tears. "This is a huge trip for me."

Paulo sighed deeply and stared silently into space. No words. He had no idea how important this time and place and journey were for her. Late-night grief transformed into a celebration of a beautiful life cut short. Realizing dawn was fast approaching, and with it a new day and more diving, Kimi bid Paulo goodnight.

"Tomorrow," Paulo said, "you will see why your friend yearned to visit."

Dawn broke and no one stirred. Finally, roused by the jubilant noises of playing children, Kimi pulled herself out of her stupor. Nursing the headaches that always accompany an over-indulgence of red wine, we ventured across the street to the neighborhood café. Even hungover, we could sense the shift. The conversation of the previous night now defined our purpose. Honoring the memory of Kimi's friend would permeate every activity. No more 4 a.m.s — timelines ceased to matter. 'Normal' became wake up late, laze around, rally over coffee, and then make their way to the water to gather ingredients for an evening feast. Instead of majestic pelagic tunas, Kimi and Paulo hunted humble limpets and octopus in the shallows. The lone hunters became a family of gatherers. Freed from the mental strain of searching for trophy fish, meal prep dominated the majority of our days. The laughter returned as Kimi and Paulo marveled over the remarkable

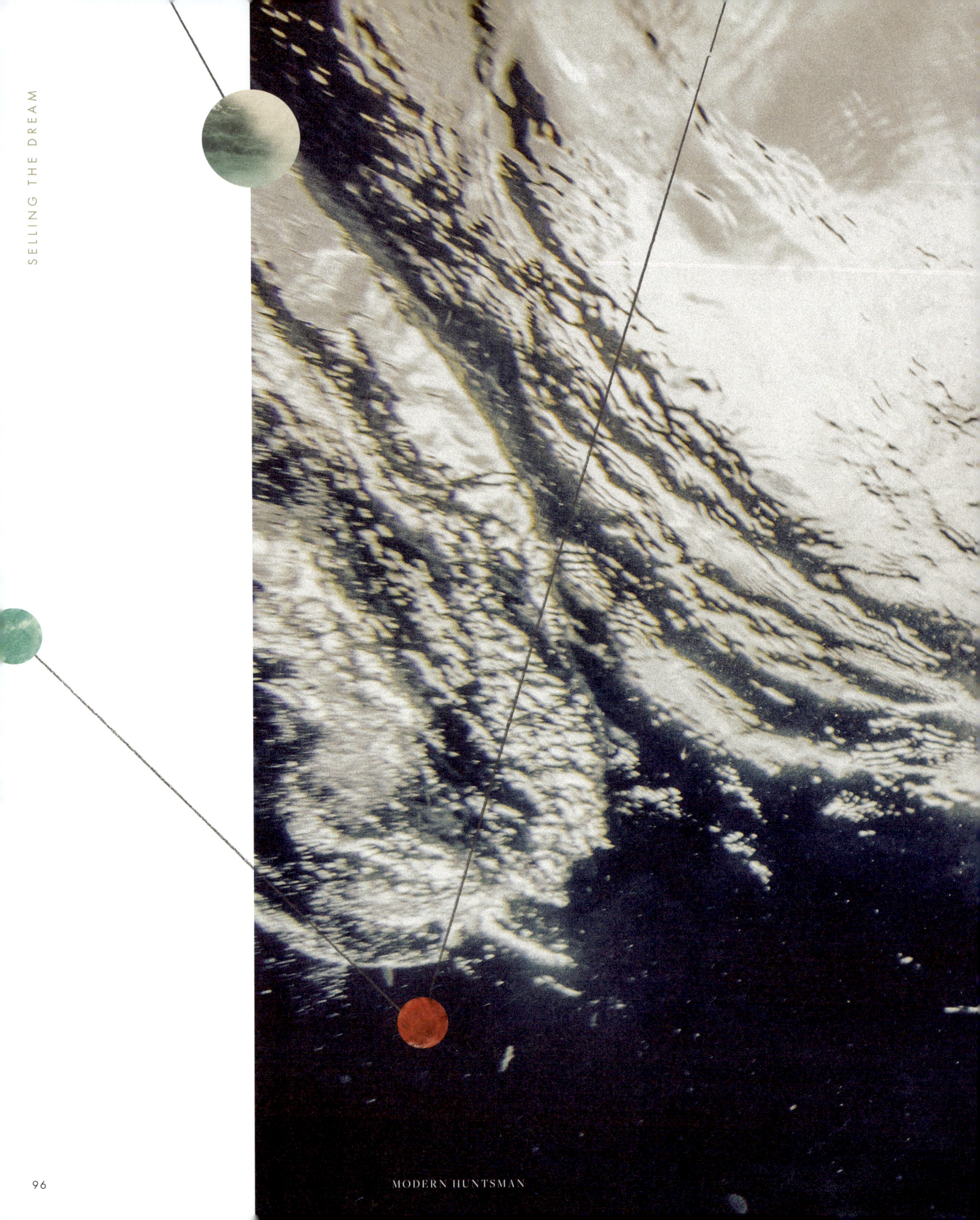

DJ STRUNTZ

similarities between Hawaiian and Azorean ingredients and cuisine. Dinner remained a late-night affair, but now it wasn't a mechanical, biological urge for fuel, it was a culinary festival. Joy shone brightly in the eyes of the three generations of Azoreans and their guests seated around the rough-hewn table. Heaping piles of fried baitfish, boiled shore crabs, and garlic-roasted limpets stood no chance. Wine flowed once again, and stories were embellished.

Paulo was visibly relieved by the change. This pace wasn't novel to him — it was simply his everyday life. Rushing was reserved for when he could see the tuna jumping a stone's throw from his office window. Then and only then would his heightened predatory response kick into overdrive. The frenetic attempts to force this issue had unbalanced the natural rhythm here. His smile, as Kimi and his family loafed, doing not much of anything, told the true story. This was the Azores. Fish came and went, much like the violent winter gales, but what made this place so special was the deep connections between the people and their sea.

A fisherman at the harbor remarked that Paulo must be a man of great faith. When pressed as to why, his answer was simple and revealing — "Because why else would a man venture into the sea on a quest for 'the big one,' day after day?"

The old man was missing something, though. It isn't what is taken home in a tangible form that matters. It's the sum of all the little moments that make every day on the water, in the mountains or in the woods so special. Sure, it's great to bring home dinner or that once-in-a-lifetime catch, but hunting means so much more. Call of the wild, lure of the sea — it has different names, but they all are trying to capture the same experiential truth. Humans are built with an insatiable need for adventure and camaraderie. If the connection to these places and the bonds formed with those who share the journey are denied, something internal withers and dies.

Kimi was now part of this family and this place. Adopted. Regrounded. Refocused. Boarding her plane home, she turned and took one last look at the little island that had become her sanctuary. Pico might just be a speck on the map, but it had become huge in her heart. Returning home to Maui would be different this time. Rather than unpacking, repacking and heading back out on the next adventure, it was time to change the paradigm. Yes, sponsor obligations would have to be met, a girl's gotta eat, but it was time to press pause and spend time with her own family — to rebond with home and her loved ones.

DJ STRUNTZ

THE FORGOTTEN

PRESENTED BY — **EPIC PROVISIONS**

ABOVE —Nat Love, *In My Fighting Clothes*

Words by EMILÉ ZYNOBIA *Photos by* IDRIS SOLOMON

If you happen to find yourself in Rosenberg, Texas, a timeworn town spilling southwest from Houston's modern sprawl, I suggest a pit stop. On the corner of Third St. and Avenue I lies an unpretentious strip of stores. There, right smack dab in the center of them, rests a stockpile of unsung history — the Black Cowboy Museum. Beyond the front door of glass framed by electric blue panes lies a history long overdue for collective recognition. This history acknowledges the memory of a nascent West brimming in multiculturalism.

COWBOYS

TEXAS RANGERS
SLAVE PATROL
RANGERS
BOUNTY

As a Black woman who spent more than my fair share of time living in Wyoming's Western range, I've always been drawn to the richness and texture of the life that can be wrested from this unforgiving terrain. The land sculpts us to her will, not the other way around. How we stumble into the horn of plenty when we abandon the drive towards material possession. Although it's easy to romanticize, few truly experience what it means to choose this path, forging a life of hard work and lonely solace in the open range. The reality of these modern times is that few get to directly live it — this is the sole preserve of the remaining cowboys.

Stories are life blood; they are what the West and humanity at large trade in. No matter your location in this vast nation, we all grew up fattened on the iconic myths, stories and histories of the Western range. It is part of our shared identity; our collective pride and shame. The Western imagination is rapturous and devouring, but what can you do when the prevailing myths and icons don't bear any mention or resemblance to the likes of you? That is not to say I don't enjoy how my Blackness sets me apart, but rather that at times I have questioned if this "West" is mine to claim — until I found Larry Callies and his museum.

When asked why he created the Black Cowboy Museum, Larry states, "God told me to." Such a simple response veils the museum's true impact. The museum is more than an act of faith; rather, it is a prayer made manifest, aimed at reclaiming history, extending recognition, and rectifying the absence of Black presence in the Western imagination. Decades ago, when Larry discovered that Black cowboys were not solely an anomaly of his family, but rather an abundant and rich pool of characters who participated in the events of what would eventually become the Western mythos, he drank this knowledge with the quickness of parched earth. After a prematurely snuffed music career, post-divorce, and with three grown children, Larry dedicated the remainder of his life savings to the purpose of quenching us all of our ignorance.

Suited up in his Wranglers and sponsor-riddled rodeo shirt, Larry is no different than any other cowboy casually spinning the yarns of his youth. He starts his tour of the museum with a framed collage that pays pictorial homage to his bright and all-too-brief country music career. Though cowboying is in his blood, Larry's first dream was to follow in the steps of Charley Pride, a Black man who broke ground and rose to the Country Music Hall of Fame in the '60s. Larry just about made it, too. With George Strait, known as the "King of Country," as his manager, and having performed for George Bush Sr. and alongside the likes of Travis Tritt, Selena, and Emilio Navaira, it wasn't long before Larry was offered an opportunity to record at MCA Records in Nashville. The dream went belly-up upon the discovery that his voice was deteriorating. A condition of vocal dysphonia caused a tightly strained, cracking pitch in his voice. Today, although he feels like invisible hands are clenching his neck, Larry remains steadfast in his desire to speak up.

Larry is a born entertainer and storyteller, two traits that contribute to his magic as an absorbing historical guide. His charisma is made all the more apparent in his graceful detailing of the more morally reprehensible aspects of our American history — particularly as it pertains to Black and Native peoples. The relationship between a master and slave has scorched Larry's family tree, and as such he has long acknowledged the more bleak and haunting roots of our American history. His entangled lineage equips him to hold the fuller spectrum of human nature, a tacit understanding that nothing in our history is as simple as black and white. Larry does not shy away from complexity; Larry lives to color in the details.

Texas is the original seat of the American concept of the "cowboy," a tradition greatly influenced by the Mestizo vaqueros of mixed Spanish, Latin and Indigenous ancestry — a livestock-raising heritage that preceded America and seeded present-day cowboy culture. Even more interesting is the fact that vaquero culture has roots tracing back to Moorish rule over Spain in the eighth century. Hailing from Africa, the Moors were Black Muslims whose wartime success over Spain is greatly attributed to their skilled horsemanship and breeding of hot-blooded horses. After roughly 800 years of rule, the Spanish reclaimed the Iberian Peninsula, but continued to cultivate the bloodlines begun by the Moors. Utilizing the advanced horseman skills of their former conquers, the Spanish shifted their gaze to the Americas. To this "new world," they introduced horses that gave tribes like the Comanches their wartime edge; their cattle bloodlines would eventually give us the modern Texas Longhorn. These historical narratives remind us that no single event in time exists in isolation — and there is something beautiful in this recognition. The existence of Black cowboys, all cowboys for that matter, can be traced back to the exchange of information and tools between historic European and African empires.

In the early 1820s, when Texas was still claimed as part of Mexico, white settlers began migrating to the territory with Black slaves in tow. Though Mexico disapproved of slavery, enslaved Africans were present in the territory under both Spanish and Mexican rule. In 1825, slaves accounted for about 25 percent of the settler population, which amounted to an estimated 400 to 500 enslaved individuals. According to the 1860 census, that number would shoot up to 182,566 slaves. Despite the confusing mixture of conflict and a changing overlay of territorial ownership, this region of Texas relied heavily on Black labor prior to its statehood in 1845, and long after slaves became freedmen on June 19, 1865.

When one enters the Black Cowboy Museum, an enlarged black-and-white photograph immediately lassoes the gaze. In the image stands Henry Jones, the ancestral owner of one of the oldest white-owned settlements in Texas, the Jones Ranch. Behind Jones sit six Black men comfortably atop horses. Notably, one man has a brand in hand, indicating that these men were tending to cattle. The image is dated in the 1880s. One hundred and thirty years later, that same ranch would become the George Ranch Historical Park, where Larry worked giving tours and telling the stories of these Black cowboys.

The remarkable thing about this photo is how unremarkable Black cowboys were in 1880s Texas. In pre-Civil War Texas, slaves were commonly found on horseback, riding the open range to gather up the abundance of unbranded wild longhorn cattle left over from abandoned Spanish settlements. The combination of dense, thorn-laden mesquite and chaparral thickets and the taxing Texas heat made cattle-gathering grinding work. Though ranchers also bred cattle, it's estimated that five to six million Longhorns once grazed wild throughout the sparsely populated Texas of the late 1860s. These conditions created a labor vacuum, which slaves and freedmen participated in filling.

Mike Searles, Professor Emeritus at Augusta State University and expert in the history of the "forgotten black cowboys," points to recorded accounts from former cowboy slaves that reveal the higher degree of rapport that many of them had with their masters. Although these cowboys remained slaves, on horseback, far beyond the overseer's gaze, they leaned into the sensory experience and temporary independence cattle gathering yielded. In fact, these "cow hunters" typically endured less bondage, donned better clothing, and regularly ate meat. This was due to a combination of factors; cowboy slaves had a high degree of skill on horseback, meaning they had value to their masters, and also, according to Searles, "how you treat someone on horseback is different, because of how easy it would be for a slave to run away." During the Civil War, when many white landowners took up arms for the Confederacy and headed east, it was slaves who maintained their ranches and cattle.

A confluence of factors allowed Black cowboys to persist post-enslavement. With the end of the Civil War in 1865, ranches were suddenly without the free labor they relied upon. This moment coincided with an increase in a national demand for beef, breathing fresh vigor into what became the height of the Texas cattle drives — a fountainhead of the Western cowboy myth. From 1866-1900, knowledgeable slave cowboys seamlessly transitioned into paid work as cowboys. Strikingly, it was not uncommon for paid cowboys to work for the same ranches under which they'd been formerly enslaved. It is estimated that between eight and nine thousand Black men worked as cowboys during this period. Though the number of Black cowboys was always greatest in the Texas Gulf Coast, their presence across the Western expanse was, by all accounts, about as noteworthy as a tumbleweed.

The very nature of frontier living breeds a quality of egalitarianism; the frontier and the edges of expansion rest most on skill and effort and least upon the color of one's hands. That is not to say the frontier was in any way an ideal archetype for a diverse and equitable society, but confronted with the demands of survival, our ties to prejudice are less tightly bound. Yes, racism was omnipresent, especially in the attitudes, laws, and institutions that actively pursued Black disenfranchisement and exclusion, but as historian Kenneth Wiggins Porter states, "during the

Wrangler

Wrangler
BCM
Black Cowboy Museum
DEPUTY

Much of the historical literature on Black cowboys describes recorded accounts affirming them as highly regarded cowmen. From riding to roping, gathering, and branding, Black cowboys participated in all aspects of cattle management. Whether out of their own accord, implicit pressure or because they were asked, these men frequently took on the more dangerous and arduous tasks.

---

halcyon days of the cattle range, Blacks there frequently enjoyed greater opportunities for a dignified life than anywhere else in the United States."

Much of the historical literature on Black cowboys describes recorded accounts affirming them as highly regarded cowmen. From riding to roping, gathering and branding, Black cowboys participated in all aspects of cattle management. Whether out of their own accord, implicit pressure or because they were asked, these men frequently took on the more dangerous and arduous tasks. Black cowboys were near the bottom of social hierarchies, and so they had to exercise great skill and doggedness to avoid being replaced. The records tell of how they swam the swollen rivers ahead of the cattle, took the first pitch out of rough horses, quelled raging stampedes, and even sang through the night to instill a sense of calm among their charges.

With such emphasis on talent, it's unsurprising that more than a few achieved widespread acclaim for their accomplishments. Two commonly referenced Black cowboys are "Bulldogging" Bill Pickett and "Deadwood Dick" Nat Love; the mainstream popularity of their respective stories is, however, the exception and not the rule. The novel Lonesome Dove entails the trials of a cattle drive and the deep bond between a white trail boss and a Black cowboy. This is not merely a fictional story, but rather underscores a lived history. Charles Goodnight, a trail boss from Texas, did indeed travel for many years with a trusted black cowboy by the name of Bose Ikard. In one example of established faith, Goodnight often entrusted large sums of money to Ikard on the trail. When Goodnight learned of Ikard's passing, he purchased a stone to adjoin his grave with a statement that read, "Bose Ikard served with me four years on the Goodnight-Loving Trail, never shirked a duty or disobeyed an order, rode with me in many stampedes, participated in three engagements with Comanches, splendid behavior."

Many Black cowboys have been immortalized in a litany of films, books, essays and art. As early as 1937, films like *Harlem on the Prairie* aimed to remind Americans that black people were present in the American West. Later, in the '70s and into the '90s, we had films like *Buck and the Preacher*, *Buffalo Soldiers*, and *Posse*. Philip Durham and Everett L. Jones' book *Negro Cowboys* is one of the earliest texts to cover the extensive involvement of Blacks in the west. These works have tried, time and time again, to wake society to the fact that Black cowboys were as much a part of the West as their iconized white peers. Still, they remain largely forgotten by mainstream culture. Larry's museum is emblematic of our need to reflect and better understand how our past and present are inextricably linked, and how the confluence of the two dictate our future. Such a trove of American history raises the questions. Who gets to be iconic? Can our historical imagination ever be righted? Why did the story of the Black cowboy disappear?

A few factors contributed to the omission of Black cowboys from the American imagination. First and foremost is a mixture of timing and exclusion. By the 1920s, when the sun began to rise for the fictionalized Western epics and character legends that we know today, the dust kicked up by the genuine events of the West had long since settled — the massive cattle drives of the 1880s were a distant memory. The writers who came to cover the exploits of an old West knew that literary grandeur was the only lucrative path, and America was living through a period where all her heroes were white. Racism did not allow for genuine interest in the sharing of Black men's stories. As a consequence, the dime store comic books, followed later by the phenomenon of Western films, told the stories of white heroes in the West. At best, these narratives ignored the existence of Black cowboys, and at their most cutting, they replaced historical Black figures with fictionalized white heroes. What we are left with is a caricature of the real West, whitewashed so that we can never know the full impact of America's Black cowboys. As Black cowboy historian Philip Durham wrote, the non-white cowboy was "confronted with a color line over which he could not ride."

Another factor that contributed to the forgotten history of Black cowboys was the boom and consecutive bust of the cattle industry. The pinnacle era of the cattle kings and lucrative cattle drives began to decline in the 1880s due to overgrazing, the decreasing profitability of beef, the railway system, and the onset of refrigeration. There were fewer and fewer cowboy posts to take up, and many of the Black cowboys lost out to their white counterparts. It was not uncommon for Black cowboys, picking up on the shifting times, to become Pullman porters on trains. Even Nat Love discusses this transition in his autobiography, from riding through the dust on horseback to the "iron horse and steel road."

It is difficult to pierce the engrossing fantasy of the modern cowboy myth. The very heart of the cowboy appeal is sourced from the anonymity of real people and the ingloriousness of the

labor. The sense of nobility surrounding this work is born out of the many nameless people who collectively shouldered what was considered undistinguished labor. During the height of the cattle drives, there was nothing glorious about being a cowboy; it was hard, tough work in which many men, no matter their color partook. That the labor was considered unremarkable in its time also contributed to the disappearance of the Black cowboy.

The Black Cowboy Museum and the artifacts housed in this three-room building in Rosenberg, Texas remind us that Black cowboys were not only part of the historic West, but are still an integral part of the landscape today.

In one moment, Larry shares with me how a painted image of him sitting atop his horse during a rodeo sold for a high number at auction, and has been printed over three thousand times. Then, Larry points to his family lineage, containing generations of Black cowboys. He mentions always being in the shadow of his father, Leon "Puggy" Callies, and his uncle, "Big Preacher" Williams, and how they taught him everything about cowboying and roping. They were true rodeo cowboys who competed in saddle bronc riding, calf roping, and steer dogging events at all-Black rodeos. His first cousin, Tex Williams, is a rodeo legend in his own right. Tex became the first Black man to win the Texas State High School Finals in 1967.

Larry's stories don't come close to ending there. First put atop a horse at three years old, Larry spent much of his childhood working and gentling cattle for rodeo. As an adult, he worked with his father for infamous Texas stock producer Sloan Williams, where he was responsible for a number of Texas Rodeo Hall of Fame bucking bulls. From raising cattle to working in rodeos and moonlighting as a saddle maker, he has just about done it all. His reels of personal stories call to mind a quote from arguably the most iconic Black cowboy, Nat Love, recounting his "love of showing off" and how it's "a weakness of all cowboys more or less."

One thing is clear upon visiting the Black Cowboy Museum; the man does not stand apart from the museum. Larry is a cowboy in his own right.

One evening, after the heat of the day settled, we walked behind his home to greet his two high-withered horses, Tank and Swamper, who were grazing on the tall Texas grass. We saddled up and rode the quiet back roads through the neighboring ranches. He talked about how being a Black man in Texas has changed over the decades, and the many ways it hasn't changed at all. He still sings despite his vocal dysphonia, putting music to poems he finds. Later, he picked up his guitar to play one for me, and even through the moments where the hearing gets rough, it is Larry's unrelenting spirit to go on, to not be silenced that leaves the most profound signatures as he sings.

When it comes to the omission of Black cowboys from the Western story, you won't find bitterness spitting from Larry's lips. He possesses a graceful, albeit pained acceptance, that "that was just the way it was," and yet he remains undeterred in his conviction that these histories must still be told. Herein lies the vital purpose of a museum such as Larry's: history is passed down like a life-sustaining hardtack. Though unadorned and incomplete, this acts as a transference of knowledge in the multigenerational endeavor to combat legacies of erasure. If we as a society are able to fold a more complete picture of historical reality into our contemporary minds, then perhaps we can imagine a future befitting of our intertwined fortunes. Larry imparts his intent above the exit of the museum for all to read: "According to an African proverb, until the lion tells his side of the story, the tale of the hunt will always glorify the hunter."

A MONOGRAPH

FRÉDÉRIC LAGRANGE

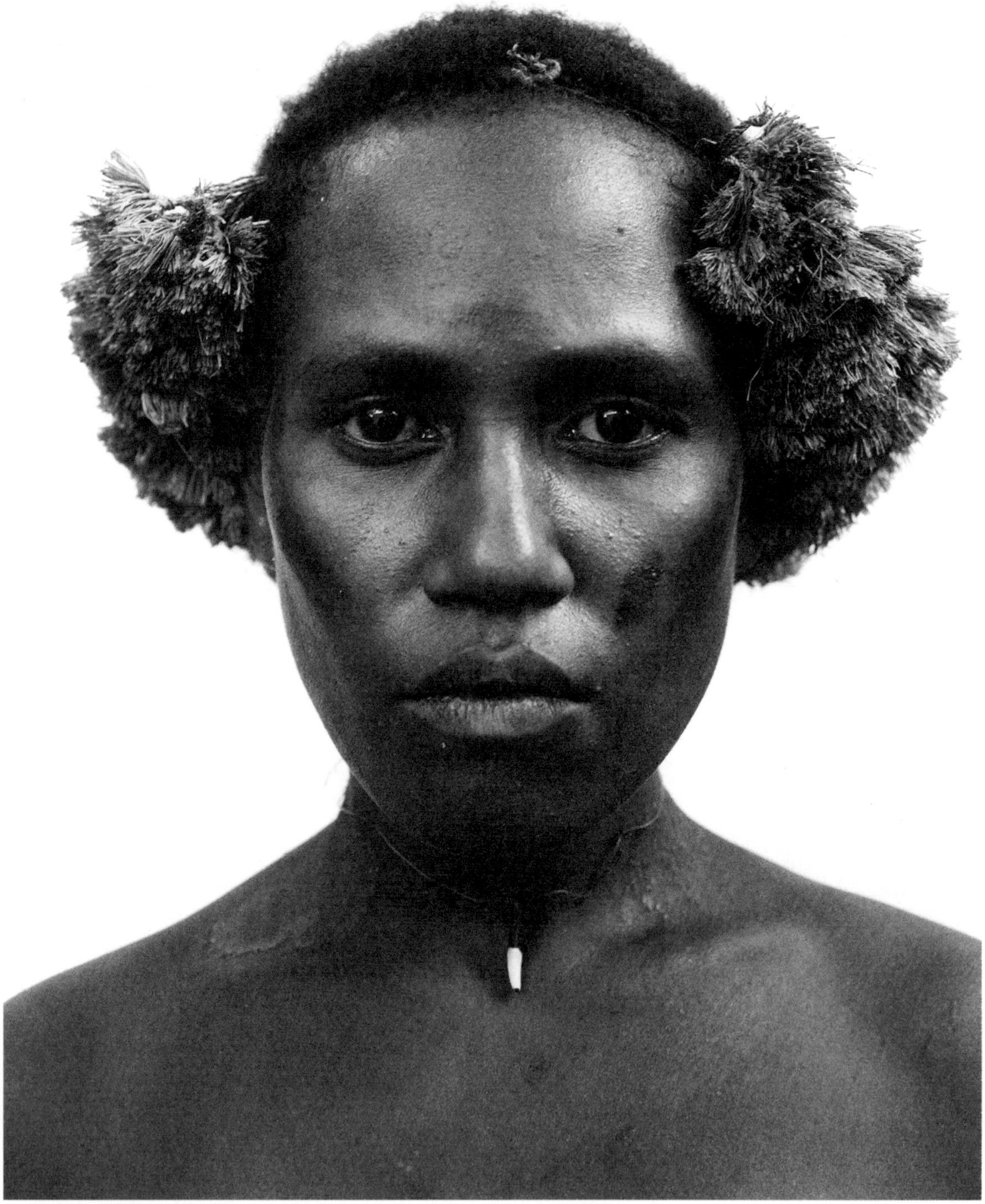

Indonesia is an archipelago of more than 17,000 islands. Over half of them are void of human presence or habitation. I first started to travel in that country in the mid 1990s, inspired by the documentary work of Laurence and Lorne Blair, two British brothers who in the early 1970s embarked on a seven-year long journey through the Indonesian archipelago in search of the 'birds of paradise.' The film that resulted, *Ring of Fire,* is an epic odyssey that displayed images of a long-gone era of thrilling adventures in far corners of a fascinating and intriguing country. Papua, or Irian Jaya as it's also called, is probably one of the least explored islands in the archipelago, with an incredible dense flora and rich, diverse fauna. As recently as 1998, Reuters reported that two previously unknown tribes, the Aukedate and the Vahudate, had been encountered by missionaries.

As a young photographer, the fantasy of a 'first contact' encounter lured my mind, and in 2008 I joined an expedition with three other Americans in search of the Kombai tribes — a journey taking us to the highlands of the rainforest close to Wanggemalo in central Papua. I flew from Bali to Jayapura, then to Wamena where I boarded a six-seater Cessna that took our tour group to the tiny village of Wanggemalo. At the end of the airstrip, a few dozen half-dressed members of the Kombai tribe were patiently waiting for this rare arrival. They were going to be our guides for the next two weeks trekking through the rainforest. The goal of our expedition was to meet forest-dwelling Kombai who had never seen this airstrip; people who knew little or nothing about the modern world.

Limited writing exists on the Kombai, and it is difficult to get any historical information or references. Many of them do not live in villages, but in single family-built tree houses high above the forest canopy that is supposed to protect them from potential enemies. Papua is the last wild and untamed place in Indonesia and probably one of the least settled in the world, having seen very few farmers or prospectors. The interior feels very cloistered.

At dawn, on the morning of our departure into the interior, a column of porters almost a third of a mile long formed. They carried weapons, tent bags, cooking supplies and food. We left the swamps and entered the dense forest, with the canopy blocking out the sky and sun. The heat was intense and I was covered with deet to protect me from malarial mosquitoes. In contrast, our Kombai guides navigated the forest effortlessly. Toward the end of the day, we reached our first treehouse. The scene was surreal. We were standing at the edge of a sun-flooded clearing with the debris of a hundred shattered trees. At its centre, a house on stilts stood 20 metres off the ground. The owner of the house, a man I assumed to be in his 40s, began walking toward us, a look of anxiety on his face. He was holding a bow and a meter-long sugarcane arrow. To defuse the tension, one of our Kombai guides pulled out a bag of Indonesian tobacco and approached the trembling man. After a few moments and a brief conversation, from a distance, we saw him smile and lower his arrow to the ground. We camped near his tree house on that first night. As we got deeper and deeper into the forest, the next two weeks were filled with similar encounters with different Kombai families, each distinctively intense, a succession of utterly beautiful moments.

My time with the Kombai people was humbling. I think about them still from time to time, about the harsh conditions in which they live, the primordial forest and life where we all come from.

— FRÉDÉRIC LAGRANGE

P.111 Details of a necklace with dog teeth around a Kombai hunter's neck, deep in the rain forest close to Wanggemalo, Iran Jaya, Indonesia.

P.112 A mother is carrying a child through the forest in a bag made of rattan.

P.113 Kombai hunter with his bow and arrows.

P.114 A woman standing against a giant sago palm.

P.115 Three Kombai women wearing bushy skirts made of sago fiber.

P.116 Looking down on a rugged river valley from a chartered Cessna on the way to Wanggemalo.

P.117 Kombai hunter carrying a dead wild pig he had just hunted.

P.118 A Kombai tree house.

P.119 Bofoko, one of the Kombai hunters who guided us through the rain forest, taking in the view from a tree house.

P.120 Kombai woman posing with a headdresses made of woven sago-palm fiber.

P.121 Kombai hunter with a necklace made of dog teeth.

P.122 View of the dense rain forest.

ON THE WINGBEATS OF BUTTERFLIES

Story by BYRON PACE

Cradled in the glow of burning coals, spitting, tortured timber spat its life history into the air, each floating ember choreographing its final dance. On the wall above the fireplace, rods and reels remained as dry as they had been all season; cold steel and married walnut lay dormant, clean and at peace. This was not a conscious decision. It had merely been a function of life. With the verdant flora of summer bowing to the russet vibrance of fall, I found myself mulling over the opportunities of seasons left. What did I want from them? My dog and companion, already old and embracing retirement, might see three more summers. At best I could hope for thirty with the same capabilities I have now.

BELOW — Chauvet-Pont-d'Arc Cave paintings, southeastern France

Contemplation of purpose can present us with equal enlightenment and darkness — what is the human existence if it is not to find purpose? If we discover this in the pursuit of knowledge, "what is the purpose of knowledge, or the drive to enquire, if not to improve one's own situation?"[1] Biologist and conservationist Alistair Graham expanded on his profound question by identifying that the 'biological function' of knowledge is the enhancement of our capability to exploit the environment around us. Crucially, this is only of benefit for those who need more than they already have — and thus the paradox of what we define as 'progress.' Graham's cultural and social observations of the Turkana people on the banks of Lake Rudolf (now Lake Turkana), northern Kenya, offer a visceral account of our growing disconnect: we are life, so we are connected — we *are* nature. Our failure to recognise this has facilitated the merciless, unrepenting march of the systematic destruction of our home.

The oldest evidence of life in the fossil record dates 3.5 billion years old — the remnants of sun-loving cyanobacteria called stromatolites. But it wasn't until 530 million years ago that we saw the first true vertebrate body form. The oldest recorded species to sit on the human evolutionary tree was discovered in Ethiopia, an ancestor of the famed 'Lucy' species (*Australopithecus afarensis*) and dates 4.4 million years old. Modern humans, *homo sapiens*, roamed the planet from 195,000 years ago. The span of a human life today is a mere blip in the evolutionary timeline. Yet, our impact on the earth, in a single lifetime, has been unfathomable in its magnitude. Comprehension of our contribution to life on Earth is as humbling as it is terrifying. A study categorizing the total biomass of life, using carbon — the building block of all living beings — shows us that humans comprise just 0.01% of life. Indeed, within the animal kingdom — which excludes plants, bacteria, fungi, archaea and protists — we contribute just 2.5% of biomass[2], from an estimated global number of animal species of 8.7million.[3]

Beyond the functional, biological reliance we have on nature, we are beginning to understand its inextricable linkage in the fabric of humanity. Recent studies have highlighted that declines in global biodiversity go hand-in-hand with our shrinking linguistic and cultural diversity. Biodiversity hotspots and high biodiversity wilderness areas account for 70% of the languages on Earth. Research has concluded that "strong geographic concordance between biological and linguistic diversity in many areas argues for some form of functional connection."[4] A complete understanding of this is yet to be defined, but it reinforces the notion that nature has molded human evolution and cultural development.

The modern world is burdened with an incessant need, an uncontrollable desire for more than the fundamental rubric of life: to perpetuate and evolve. Our

1 Graham A, Beard P. *Eyelids of Morning.* New York Graphic Society Ltd; 1973.

2 Bar-On YM, Phillips R, Milo R. The biomass distribution on Earth. *Proc Natl Acad Sci U S A.* 2018;115(25):6506-6511. doi:10.1073/pnas.1711842115

3 Mora C, Tittensor DP, Adl S, Simpson AGB, Worm B. How many species are there on earth and in the ocean? *PLoS Biol.* 2011;9(8):1-8. doi:10.1371/journal.pbio.1001127

4 Gorenflo LJ, Romaine S, Mittermeier RA, Walker-Painemilla K. Co-occurrence of linguistic and biological diversity in biodiversity hotspots and high biodiversity wilderness areas. *Proc Natl Acad Sci U S A.* 2012;109(21):8032-8037. doi:10.1073/pnas.1117511109

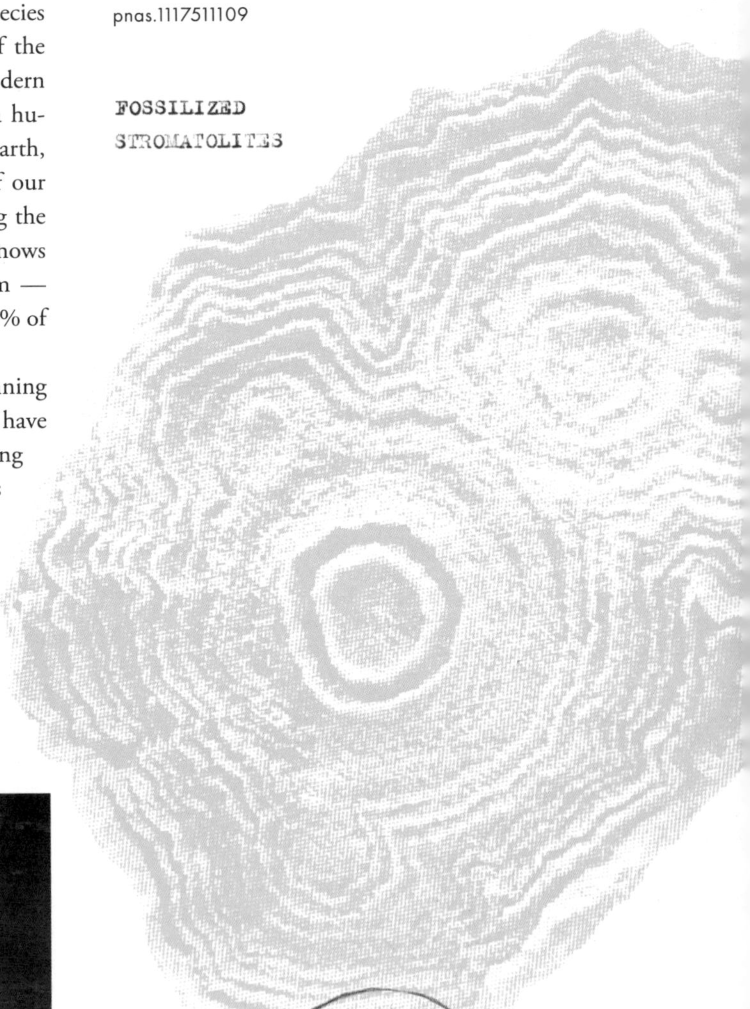

FOSSILIZED STROMATOLITES

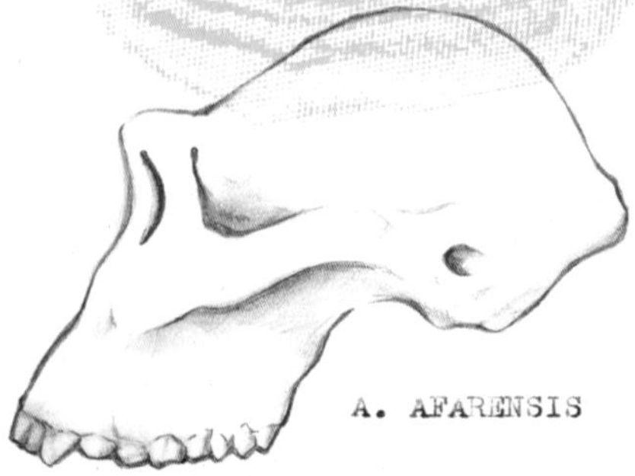

A. AFARENSIS

intelligence and the resulting advent of agriculture 12,000 years ago during the 'Neolithic Revolution' uncoupled us from the confines of nature. But this unleashed a cascade of events beyond our comprehension until recently. Our minds have made us unique among the living creatures of this planet, but propagated a belief that we are somehow ordained as the epitome of evolution. Although contemporary scholars have built on the foundational elements offered by Darwinian theory, with an Extended Evolutionary Synthesis presenting concepts including developmental bias — a prescribed trajectory for phenotypic development — what remains as true today as it did in 1859, when Charles R. Darwin unveiled *On The Origin of Species*, is that there is no pinnacle of nature's architectural design. We are only stepping stones for the next iteration of life.

Only the arrogance of humans, filled with the narcissistic tendencies of grandeur and conquest, would assume that the morphological outcome of homo-sapiens, with our constructs, philosophies, cultures and perceived importance, is the culmination of an intended result. Peter Beard, one of the keenest holistic observers of human-animal interactions, was among the first to encapsulate our failure as custodians of life on Earth with *The End of The Game*.[5] However, he was wrong in a way, as there can be no 'endgame,' because there is no end. There is no apex of life. There is only the time which preceded us, from a single-celled organism floating in a panacea of possible futures, and an unknown period stretching out into the imperceptible darkness. It's for us to create the light.

Given the frequency with which species are threatened with extinction, it's easy for the drip of information to rumble only as background noise to the cacophony of global chaos. One could even be forgiven for wondering how much it matters. Beyond those individuals with a personal connection, most of the species that fill the columns of the IUCN Red List are animals we haven't seen or heard of. How would our lives change if the Mekong giant catfish no longer swam the waterways of Southeast Asia, or the calumma tarzan chameleon disappeared from the forests of Madagascar? Barely a person on the planet would notice. However, this is a dangerous veneer of conjecture, which fails to recognise self-interest, never mind any moral obligation society bestows upon us.

We are living in the epoch of humans, the Anthropocene, and as we consider the resilience of species and ecosystems to anthropic impacts, it is ironically the resilience of our species which has led us to this contemplation. Today, we grapple with species' ability to cope with environmental shifts, as the weight of the human population bears down on every corner of the planet. From synthetic fibres in the digestive tracts of amphipods in our deepest oceans to the invasive introduction of earthworms in the Arctic, the adaptability of humans has been to the detriment of all other life on Earth.

The importance of understanding these impacts is rapidly being laid at our door. We are breaking natural cycles that have provided the unique environmental stability of the Holocene — the current geologic epoch spanning from the end of the last ice age, 11,700 years ago, to the present. Our oceans are acidifying, degrading coral reefs and fisheries; extreme weather events continue to increase, bringing fire and flooding in equal measures; and as our soils degrade, reducing yields and productivity, we continue to breach the few remaining wild spaces. This is not just a story of saving the *other* life on the planet; it's one of *our* survival.

As altruistic as we can endeavour to be, the conservation of species, even if seemingly for their intrinsic value, will never be the foundational motivation. We will always make a trade for marginal benefit, and this will be for the perceived betterment of our well-being. It is inescapable, and crucially the reason we need to encompass the real value of ecosystem services offered by restoring biodiversity.

In tackling this as a global responsibility, it's fundamental that we understand what we are trying to achieve. The concept of biodiversity has undoubtedly come to the fore in the last decade, but it is inherently difficult to value and measure, and often poorly understood. In a survey before the 2010 'Year of Biodiversity' set by the United Nations,

5 Beard P. *The End of The Game.* Taschen; 1963.

GLOSSARY

Amphipods: *describe a group comprising of thousands of shrimp-like species, which are often determined as keystone in their ecosystem.*

Phenotype: *the observable characteristics of an organism.*

Extended Evolutionary Synthesis: *a concept of evolutionary theory which builds on the foundations of Darwin and incorporates modern science and understanding.*

Developmental bias: *a concept which explains how evolutionary development is not entirely random, but can show examples of parallel evolution with commonality in certain traits between species which evolved independently.*

Differences in intra-species gene expression: *how genes within the same species can provide a variety of information to cells, and hence why some individuals in the threatened frogs described were able to survive the effects of the pathogen.*

Archaea: *single-celled organisms with structures similar to bacteria. They are found in some of the most inhospitable environments on the planet.*

Protists: *organisms usually comprising a single cell, or a colony of cells, living primary in water.*

members of the public were asked what they understood biodiversity to mean. The most common answer: "some kind of washing powder." How can we protect something if we don't know what it is?

In 2010, the Conference of the Parties (COP) for the Convention on Biological Diversity (CBD), established the twenty Aichi Biodiversity Targets, with an overarching vision for a world "living in harmony with nature." A decade later, we are facing the failure to fulfill a single complete target. We have been here before. The 2010 conference was a restructuring of strategies on the inability to meet the 2002 commitments, for "a significant reduction of the current rate of biodiversity loss at the global, regional, and national level as a contribution to poverty alleviation and to the benefit of all life on earth." One could say we are adept at having meetings and writing minutes and poor at implementing action.

Scanning down the *Global Biodiversity Outlook 5* (GBO) summary paper, the repetitive nature of reading "the target has not been achieved" can only leave a depressing, sinking feeling. Despair may be difficult to quell, but we must, for we have no choice but to forge on, learn from our failures and focus efforts on the future.

There are, however, embers of optimism from the cauldrons of anguish. Progress has been made, with expansions of protected areas in both terrestrial and marine environments, with Key Biodiversity Areas (KBA) expanding from coverage of 29% to 44% in the last decade. The GBO report estimates that without the implementation and progress across targets, we would have seen "extinctions of birds and mammals in the past decade likely to have been two to four times higher." Even though our current extinction rates are estimated to be around a thousand times more than the background rate, we must acknowledge this would have been worse without action.

However, caution and critical thinking should always be applied. When we read that deforestation *globally* has "fallen by a third when compared to the previous decade," it is essential to question if forest cover offsets are proportional for supporting biodiversity — they invariably are not. It's well established that tropical regions of the world support the greatest diversity of life. Forest cover in the UNECE region of the northern hemisphere — an area of 47 million square kilometres across 56 countries — grew by the size of the United Kingdom between 2000 and 2015. On the face of it this is a positive move, although it doesn't strip out plantations of poor biodiversity value, such as prevalent non-native Sitka spruce in the U.K. On the other hand, despite the positive note from the United Nations GBO report on deforestation, The World Resource Institute in 2019 still reported a reduction in the world's primary rainforest by an area the size of Belgium. The data provided by Global Forest Watch shows a steady trend of tropical primary forest loss starting in the early 2000s, with a spike in 2016 and 2017 predominantly due to increased fire.

Biodiversity encapsulates an infinitely complex, intricate flow of relationships between organisms. Sustaining this requires a long-term vision of deliberate management, and a realization that we cannot simply compensate by substitution.

The most all-encompassing evaluation for life on Earth comes from the Living Planet Index, updated in the comprehensive 2020 version of the World Wildlife Fund (WWF) *Living Planet Report*. The index tracks more than 21,000 populations of mammals, birds, fish and reptiles, representing their trend with a starting point of 1970 — a date selected based on information availability. This shows an average rate of decline across the planet of 68% over the last fifty years, with a confidence interval of +/-5%. The largest contributing factor: changes in land and sea use for agriculture, logging, energy production and development.

Breaking this down a little further, it becomes clear that the most significant declines are being seen in the locations with the highest biodiversity. Most starkly, South America suffers a staggering 94% rate of decline across monitored species. Most of this has been in amphibians, reptiles and fish — animals which so often go unnoticed. These unassuming creatures face myriad threats, from the habitat fragmentation of hydro-dams limiting gene

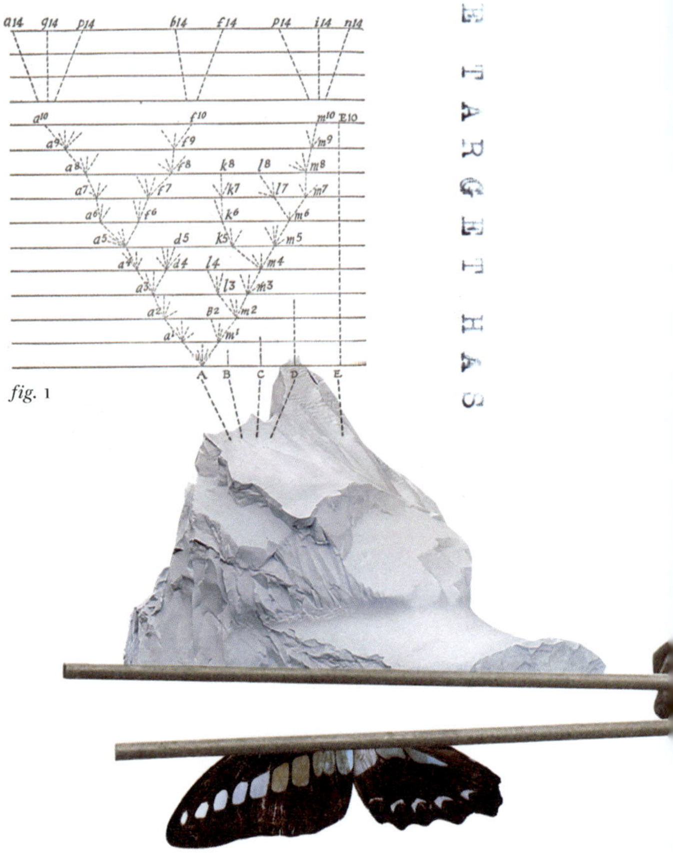

fig. 1

THE TARGET HAS NOT BEEN ACHIEVED.

fig. 1
Darwin C. *On the origin of species by means of natural selection, or, the preservation of favoured races in the struggle for life*. London, J. Murray; 1859

flow, to mass mortality resulting from diseases transported by humans. In one highland region of Panama alone, thirty species of amphibians were lost as a result of the Africa-originating chytrid fungus, *Batrachochytrium dendrobatidis* (Bd).

In this story of devastation lies an important lesson: our concern should sit not only with the abundance of species, but also with the diversity within species. Recent studies have found that intra-species gene expression may explain variations in survival of the deadly Bd pathogen. The 2010 CBD Aichi Biodiversity Targets acknowledged the importance of minimizing genetic erosion, but we still understand very little about this silent degradation within species. However, it's clear that the preservation of genetic diversity improves the resilience to shifting environmental factors.

Expanding on this, "accumulating evidence indicates that both genetic and non-genetic inheritance, and the interactions between them, have important effects on evolutionary outcomes."[7] This expanding body of work, which suggests that evolution be redefined as "the process by which the frequencies of *variants* (and not solely genes) in populations change over time," extends the potential considerations for successful conservation. These studies highlight the importance of epigenetics — heritable changes which don't involve alterations in DNA — as well as ecological, parental and cultural inheritance of species as part of the "engine of evolution." We need look no further than humans to realize the fundamental truth in this. Fascinating recent research on killer whales also points to the significance of cultural inheritance in the formation of ecotypes — members of distinct groups which tend to be extremely specialized in what they eat and how often they catch it.[8] If we are to be successful in our conservation of life on Earth, we must continue to expand our understanding of this complex web of interactions that define the makeup of existence as we know it.

By acting on the knowledge we glean from this process of scientific endeavour, we can help maintain the ability of nature to support human life: "the functions and processes of ecosystems that benefit humans"[9] — more commonly referred to as ecosystem services. From the provision of clean water to global food security and the very oxygen we breathe, the appreciation and valuation of Earth's natural capital will be fundamental in its protection.

This requires an adaptation of human psychological and philosophical thinking. We need nature far more than it needs us. Life will go on, as indeed it has five times before in the aftermath of the great extinctions.

As we consider the conservation of wildlife and protection of ecosystems, there is a tale of caution as we rise from the rubble of ruins; a challenge conservationists have faced for decades, and articled in stunning eloquence by Alistair Graham in his book *Eyelids of Morning*.

"And when the wilderness has been sold out, the inevitable remorse will set in. But that which has been obliterated can never be reconstituted. It cannot be remade as a national park, because gazetted paradises are as artificial as the laws behind them, the sentiments around them, and the robots within them."

The earth is our eternal, all-providing mother, and her beating heart is the web of life, infinitely connected in continuous and overlapping eco-evolutionary feedback loops. Humans are part of this. Long-term, successful conservation will not solely come from reducing our footprint on the planet. It will equally require integrating people within wild spaces, syncing symbiotically in our relationship and ability to harvest wild food and resources. Embracing indigenous knowledge is key and will nurture the evolution of the modern hunter: part naturalist, anthropologist, conservationist and philosopher.

Darkness is always present in the absence of light, and it is for humans to emerge from the chrysalis of illuminated thought, reforging the trajectory of our time, to rise with the enduring, elucidated grace of a butterfly — offering to the world more than we take.

6 Eskew EA, Shock BC, Ladouceur EEB, et al. Gene expression differs in susceptible and resistant amphibians exposed to batrachochytrium dendrobatidis. *R Soc Open Sci.* 2018;5(2). doi:10.1098/rsos.170910

7 Danchin É, Charmantier A, Champagne FA, Mesoudi A, Pujol B, Blanchet S. Beyond DNA: Integrating inclusive inheritance into an extended theory of evolution. *Nat Rev Genet.* 2011;12(7):475-486. doi:10.1038/nrg3028

8 Whitehead H. Gene–culture coevolution in whales and dolphins. *Proc Natl Acad Sci U S A.* 2017;114(30):7814-7821. doi:10.1073/pnas.1620736114

9 Costanza R, de Groot R, Braat L, et al. Twenty years of ecosystem services: How far have we come and how far do we still need to go? *Ecosyst Serv.* 2017;28:1-16. doi:10.1016/j.ecoser.2017.09.008

BATOUALA

The river, always the river

COPYRIGHT/TITO WEST

Story by TITO WEST

These photographs are from a trip into the rainforest of southern Cameroon in 2016. They were taken along the Boumba River, not far from the Congo border. Of the 10 rolls of film I brought with me on the trip, almost all suffered water damage. Only a few frames were salvageable, some of which are presented here.

The only other remnants of this trip are a handful of flashback-like memories, a fragmented collection of strangely cinematic moments that are beyond my ability to organize into any sort of linear narrative. What I remember more than anything is an ever present feeling of heaviness, of darkness that plagued this expedition from day one. It was always there, but I questioned its legitimacy until our departure was stopped short, only moments from leaving the country aboard a Turkish Airlines flight to Istanbul. We had been suspected of espionage by the Cameroonian intelligence service and were whisked away from the airport in Douala in the middle of the night to a military compound deep in the heart of the city. There, we were informed of the charges being levied against us and told to present our case. A discussion took place over a matter of days and documents were presented to support our story. Ultimately we were freed and allowed to leave, but the feeling of heaviness that had permeated the trip from the start showed itself clearly in the end. I don't know what that heaviness was or why I felt it. All I know is that it was tangible and very real and I feel it still when I look at these photographs.

These memories will always remain, just as some of the parasites from the forest that had infiltrated my body will always remain with me. And yet, in many ways, I long to go back. I suppose that I finally understand what Joseph Conrad meant when he said, "It was written I should be loyal to the nightmare of my choice."

** **NOTE TO THE READER** — Neither these photographs nor my memories of the place are indicative of the country or the people, but rather, are simply a description of my singular experience there.

the forest overhead

and the light breaking through

Baka Pygmies- Piron

Loa Loa, the eye worm parasite – the old timers used to pour paraffin on their feet after crossing rivers.

The river, always the river - the forest overhead
and the light breaking through - logging trucks,
so many trees felled - salt licks - they say the AIDS
virus began here in nonhuman primates - the Pygmies -
sharpened teeth - a dark history - a French bible -
young girl at the ceremony of the Spirit of the Forest -
palm wine - drunken army officers at the border
checkpoints with malaria yellowed eyes pressing for
bribes - the forest swallows the men as they follow
a track - logging trucks overturned on forest roads,
abandoned - 7.62mm casings - the barefoot track of a
single poacher - a dead elephant - another one further
in the forest - ants, massive columns of ants -

Gaboon Vipers

Green Vipers

TITO WEST

7.62mm casings

PHOTOGRAPHED: April 2016

a track - logging trucks overturned on forest roads, abandoned
the barefoot track of a single poacher

Gorilla Skull, Cameroon

TITO WEST

TITLE: Front Track - Lowland Gorilla, Cameroon
DATE PHOTO… May 2016
DATE PR… October 2020
EDITION: N/A
NOT TO

Lowland Gorilla, Cameroon

PHOTOGRAPHED: May 2016
PRINTED October 2020
EDITION n/a

WITHOUT

the Spirit of the Forest -

Green Vipers - Gaboon Vipers - Mamba in the canopy -

2 Headed snake - front track of a Gorilla -

a swimming yellow backed duiker - Gorillas in the trees

chimpanzees in the early morning mist - a violent

scream from a silverback deep in the forest - shaking

the trees, beating his chest, then vanishing - rain,

dust, bees - a reenactment of the hunt - the bongo skull

dancing in the half light of the fire, the spirit of

the forest, the physical manifestation of their deity.

a dead elephant - another one further in

the forest - ants, massive columns of ants

The name Batoula comes from the title of a book written by an Afro-Caribbean writer named Rene Maran. The story is about a fictional kingdom in the former French colonial territory known as Ubangi-Shari, part of which covered the region where I took these photographs.

FACING PAGE — The boy lifted the Chimpanzee skull, inadvertently covering his mouth, as if he were forbidden to speak of such taboo subjects. The rain poured down his face, pooling briefly around the eye. The myth says that during times of drought, which do occur even in the rainforest, placing a chimpanzee skull in water will bring about the rains. The symbolism was inferred in retrospect. I didn't plan it, nor did he.

Baka boy w/ Chimpanzee Skull

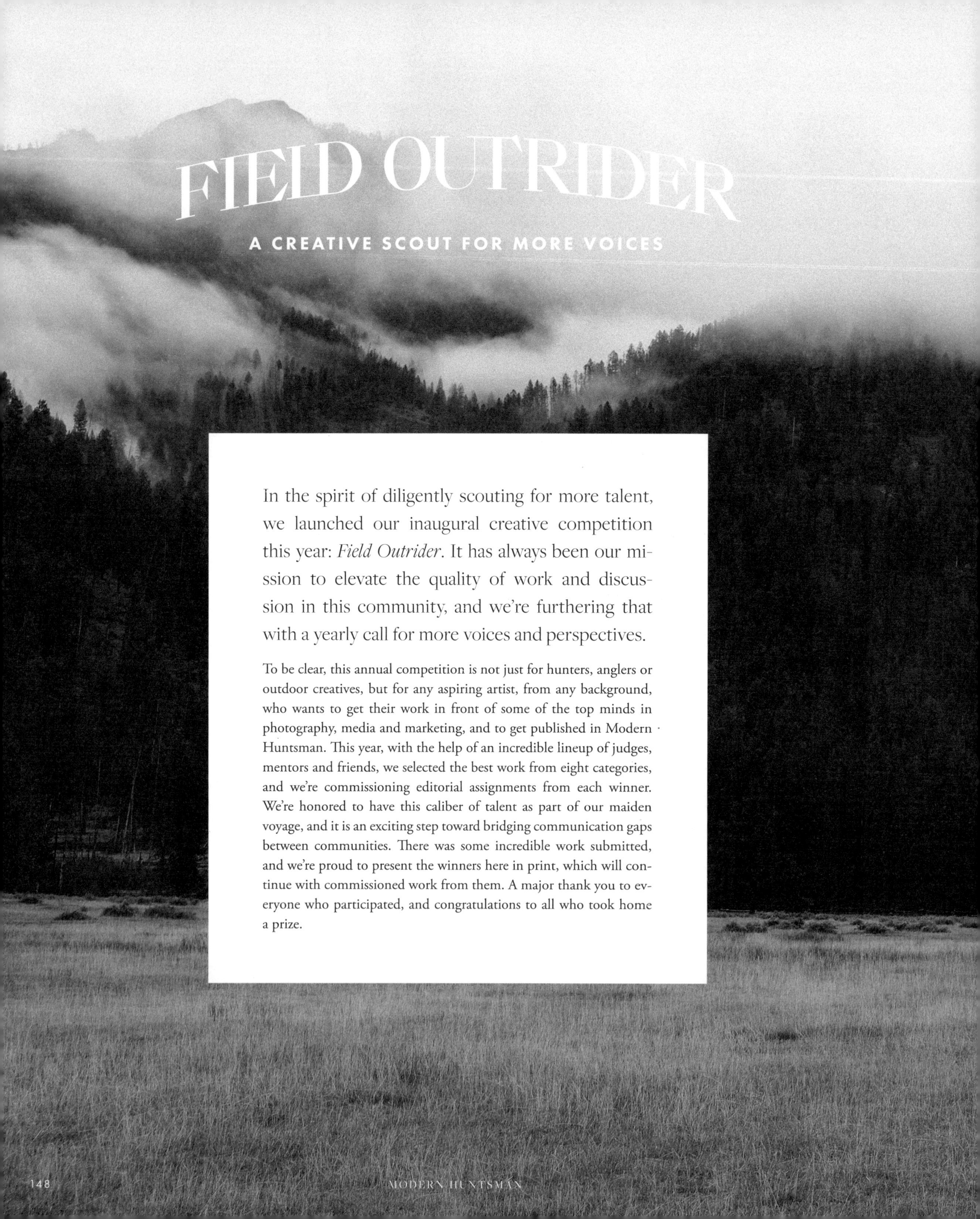

FIELD OUTRIDER

A CREATIVE SCOUT FOR MORE VOICES

In the spirit of diligently scouting for more talent, we launched our inaugural creative competition this year: *Field Outrider*. It has always been our mission to elevate the quality of work and discussion in this community, and we're furthering that with a yearly call for more voices and perspectives.

To be clear, this annual competition is not just for hunters, anglers or outdoor creatives, but for any aspiring artist, from any background, who wants to get their work in front of some of the top minds in photography, media and marketing, and to get published in Modern Huntsman. This year, with the help of an incredible lineup of judges, mentors and friends, we selected the best work from eight categories, and we're commissioning editorial assignments from each winner. We're honored to have this caliber of talent as part of our maiden voyage, and it is an exciting step toward bridging communication gaps between communities. There was some incredible work submitted, and we're proud to present the winners here in print, which will continue with commissioned work from them. A major thank you to everyone who participated, and congratulations to all who took home a prize.

ELIAS CARLSON — @ELIASCARLSON

01

CATEGORY WINNER

PURSUIT

MIKE BORCHARD — Mike is a photographer and raconteur born and raised along the coast of Southern California. Continually drawing inspiration from spearfishing, surfing, and other outdoor exploits, he has a knack for creating imagery that extolls the true feeling of people and places. He's drawn to stories with deep character — the more grit, the better. His images are heavily influenced by real life experiences and friends met along the way. The rare times when Mike isn't chasing images and stories with a camera, he's out living the stories he photographs. You might find him on a knife-edge ridge in the Ko'olau Range or 100ft underwater on a single breath. Currently, Mike splits his time between California and Hawaii.

@mikeborchard
borchardphoto.com

Spear-fisherman Barton Prideaux attempts to subdue a California bluefin tuna. Connecting yourself to a powerful fish in the middle of the ocean always comes with inherent risk: these strong fish can drag you down to the depths hundreds of feet below the surface in seconds. In this instance, a fish we thought was incapacitated got a second wind and came back to life, swimming erratically and wrapping a few loops of shooting line around Barton's legs and fins. Thankfully, this was a smaller fish. Barton was able to act quickly, controlling the fish with his legs and driving a knife through its gills and spine to dispatch it before the situation got out of hand. The process of turning a wild animal into food is never simple or clean, a truth only exaggerated when hunting on breath-hold 70+ miles offshore.

02

FIRST RUNNER UP

PURSUIT

MASON MASHON — Mason Mashon is an adventure photographer based in Whistler, BC. A pursuant of action sports in all seasons, Mason often combines harvesting from the land and the ocean to sustain himself while embedded in some of the most remote areas of British Columbia.

@mason_mashon

After a long ski tour, Rory Bushfield returns to his ski-equipped Cessna 180, nestled high and deep in the Coast Range Mountains of British Columbia. The only other tracks than our own were imprinted by a hasty wolverine wandering along the highest ridge-lines in the whole area.

03

SECOND RUNNER UP

PURSUIT

BRITTANY MCBRAYER — Brittany McBrayer is a native Texan, and has been shooting professionally for almost 11 years. Growing up on a sixth-generation cattle ranch in East Texas, she was outside for the majority of her childhood, and always loved and appreciated the pure beauty that came from the natural world. Her love affair with wildlife and landscape photography was ignited when she began spending extended time in the Jackson, WY, area each year elk hunting with her family.

@brittmcbrayer
brittmcbphoto.com

This image was taken after my dad, uncle, husband, cousin and I spent the day hunting near Moran, WY. My husband and cousin shot their bulls within an hour of each other about four miles into the backcountry. My dad and uncle pacjed both bulls out together. We didn't drag in enough pack animals for two elk, so the successful hunters got to walk out on foot. The slight haze in the image was due to fires burning in the areas around where we were hunting. I shot the image while following the pack train on my favorite mustang named Nevada. It was a perfect day I will never forget.

01

CATEGORY WINNER

HARVEST

JAY KOLSCH — Jay is a American outdoor and lifestyle photographer based in New York City. While his passion for getting outside has earned him significant commercial success, what he enjoys most is telling authentic, gritty and challenging athletic stories.

@jaykolsch
jaykolsch.com

'The world's our freezer this time of year,' Anna said, grabbing half a dozen keta salmon from two massive boxes that held an entire ton of frozen fish outside their workshop. Anna manned the chop saw, wearing work gloves, a large parka, coveralls, and safety headphones over her wool hat. The work was loud, but you could still hear 60 Alaskan huskies barking, yipping, and howling above everything. They knew exactly what the shrill of the saw meant and so did the resident bald eagle, circling above. Frozen pink crystals covered everything as the salmon pucks were dropped into two five-gallon buckets – heads, tails, and all. Kristy joined Anna in carrying them over to the team, the entire kennel jumping and shouting to make sure they all got their fair share. For the dogs, the excitement of food is second only to the anticipation of a run.

02

FIRST RUNNER UP

HARVEST

WRAY SINCLAIR — Wray's first introduction to photography was in a darkroom developing film and printing when he was 12 years old. After graduating from college, he moved to Los Angeles to pursue a career in the photo industry. Today, his work concentrates on the relationship between people and the spaces that they inhabit. Working with real people, he has an ability to connect with individuals who haven't been photographed before.

@wraysinclairphoto
wraysinclair.com

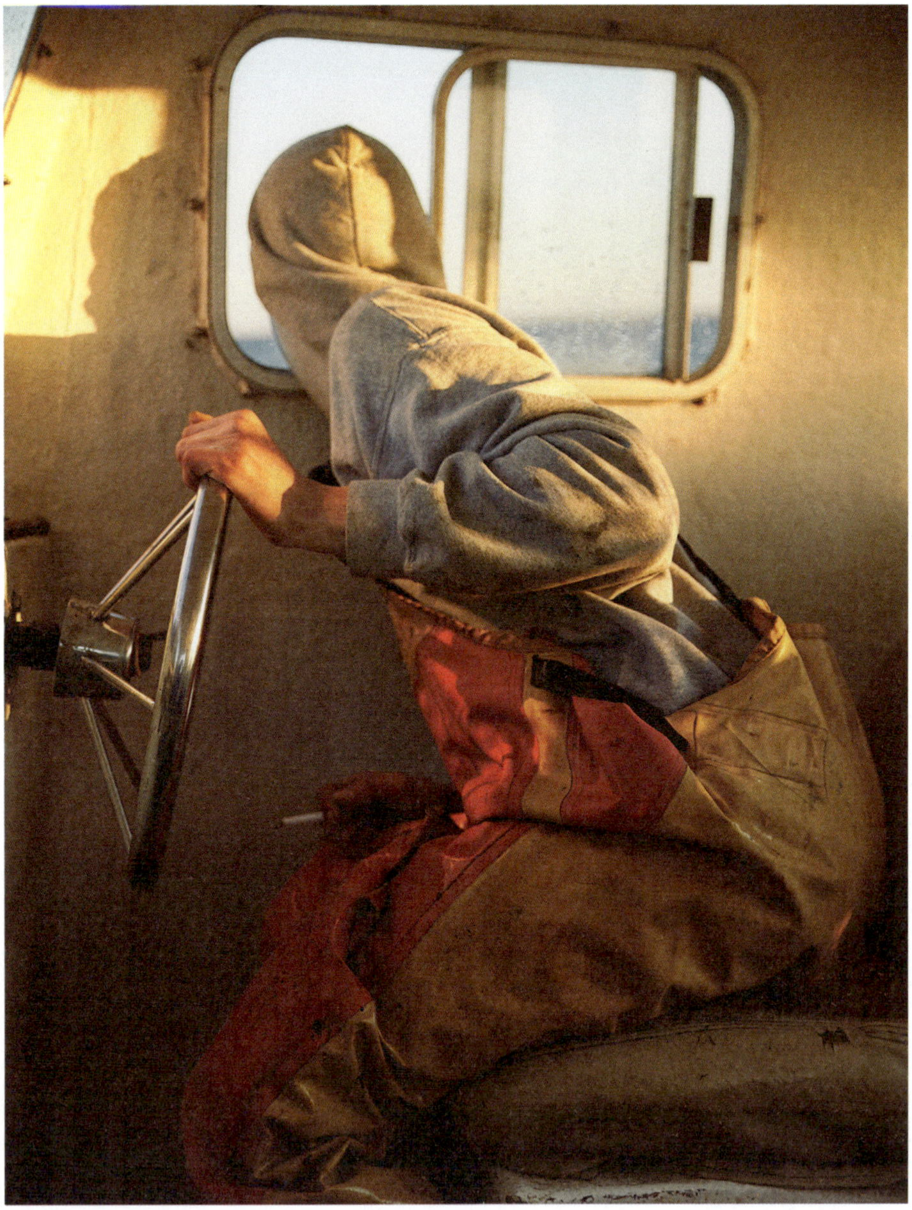

First light rises above the horizon on the Chesapeake Bay off the coast of Cape Charles, VA.
Crabbers get in position to pull a line of pots for blue crab.

03

SECOND RUNNER UP

HARVEST

JENNY NGUYEN-WHEATLEY — Jenny earned an English degree at UCLA, and shortly after, accepted a full-time position with Nebraskaland Magazine at the Nebraska Game and Parks Commission. Hunting opportunities multiplied in the Midwest, which allowed Jenny's wild game cooking and photography to grow. Born in Nha Trang, Vietnam, Jenny's cooking is heavily influenced by her Southeast Asian culture.

@foodforhunters
foodforhunters.com

This photo is an attempt to capture the transition between animal and meat, and the care that goes into it. I aged this particular pheasant in my garage for 7 days to improve its flavor, and during the tedium of plucking it, I paused to admire the transformation. With nice light streaming through my kitchen that afternoon, I dragged out my camera equipment and took one of my more interesting still life photos.

01

CATEGORY WINNER

WILD PLACES

CHRISTOPHER DOWELL — Christopher Dowell is a photographer based in Denver, CO, photographing food systems, farms, hunting, and adventure of all kinds. Originally from Chicago, IL, much of his work revolves around the Corn Belt and the tenacity of the people who farm and live there.

@christopher_dowell
missingsucks.com/art

Game trails in the snow are a brief look into the lives and minds of animals. Why a turn here, what made you run there, and where are you going? In the summer, these trails are hidden from the untrained eye, but in the winter, all is laid bare for the world to see. This image was taken in the north woods of Wisconsin while on a late winter hunting trip.

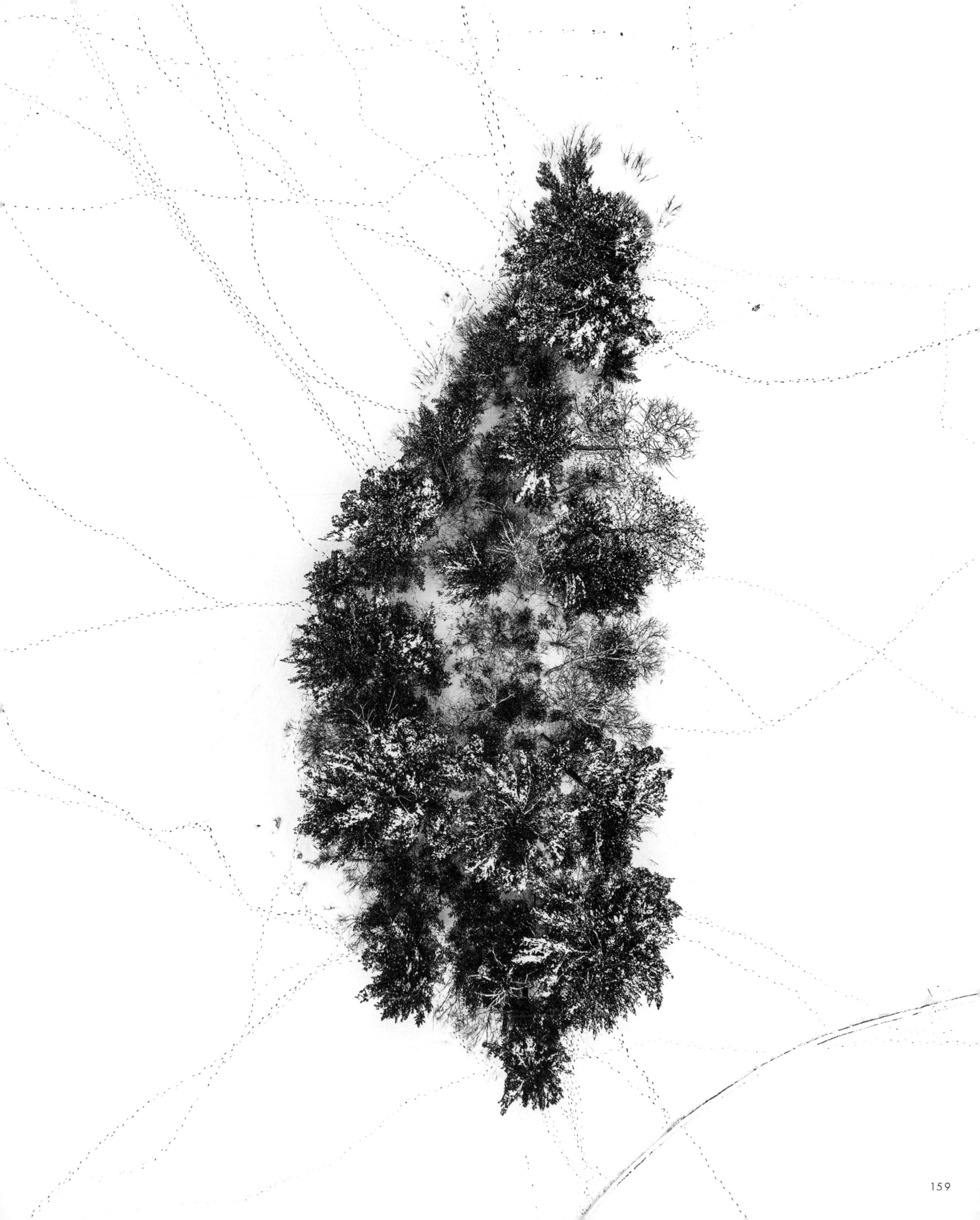

02

FIRST RUNNER UP

WILD PLACES

CALEB LETO — The outdoors have always been a big part of Caleb Leto's life. Holding a camera on his outdoor experiences keeps him going back. It's an opportunity to tell a story, and it allows him to find unique characteristics in the places he goes and the people he meets. He strives to find different perspectives in his photography, staying true to the story and the experiences in that very moment. Sharing these stories fuels his passion.

@calebleto

This image was taken shortly after a storm rolled through the Big Horn Mountains. The storm hit us 7 miles into a 14-mile day in an effort to punch a cow elk tag. Tensions were high as we watched it roll in, but we didn't expect the wind. Hunkered down under what seemed like the only four evergreen trees on the mountain, we slowly watched our footprints disappear behind us. A quick reminder to always prepare and expect the most of Mother Nature when surrounded by her beauty.

03

SECOND RUNNER UP

WILD PLACES

CLETTIS WRIGHT — Clettis Wright finds a harmonious balance between being a commercial photographer and an avid wanderer for adventure in the outdoors. He seeks to capture nature's grandeur wonderment in surreal moments in time. Gratitude and the soul-lifting experiences the outdoors have given to him carry over in his intimate imagery.

@clettis
clettiswright.com

"Where Fog Embraces the Trees in the Night"
Kawuneeche Valley Backcountry, Rocky Mountain National Park

01

CATEGORY WINNER

PORTRAITURE

SOFIA JARAMILLO — Sofia Jaramillo is an adventure and documentary photographer based out of Jackson, Wyoming. As a Colombian-American who grew up in a small mountain town, a big part of her mission is to uplift and tell the stories of BIPOC and female athletes in outdoor sports. Jaramillo got her start in photography working at newspapers and freelancing for national news outlets and transitioned to outdoor photography two years ago. She believes in the power of storytelling and with this approach has photographed for National Geographic, The North Face, Arc'Teryx and Patagonia.

@sofia_jaramillo5
sofiajaramillophoto.com

Emilé Zynobia takes a moment to reflect at Puzzleface Ranch in Wilson, Wyoming, where she learned how to ride horses as a kid.

02

FIRST RUNNER UP

PORTRAITURE

GARRETT MILANOVICH —- Originally from Florida's east coast, Garrett Milanovich is now residing in Bellvue, CO on a small farm. He currently spends much of his time documenting Colorado's rodeo scene.

@garrett_milanovich
garrettmilanovich.com

Bull riders in the calm before the storm at the Boulder County Mexican rodeo.

03

SECOND RUNNER UP

PORTRAITURE

MELANIE ELZINGA — Melanie Elzinga grew up on a cattle ranch in Idaho. She started playing with a point-and-shoot camera at a young age, learning technique through trial and error. As Melanie's photography evolved, she began using images to tell the story of her family's efforts to regenerate the Idaho rangeland on which they graze their cattle. The tenets of conservation and stewardship inform her family's everyday work, and she strives to capture that passion in her photographs.

@melzingaphoto

Every fall before the snow starts to fly, my whole family makes the drive from our ranch to the mountains to gather firewood. We take only trees killed by pine beetle or fire, clearing the forest overstory so new seedlings can regenerate in the forest ecosystem. Jeremiah Patchin rode many grueling miles on the range for us this summer, and yet we convinced him to come help with the gathering of firewood as well. He and his dog are pictured here amidst the smoke of our lunchtime campfire.

01

CATEGORY WINNER

WILDLIFE

ERIC FISHER — Eric Fisher is an avid wildlife photographer who works each summer as a fly fishing and brown bear viewing guide in Alaska. The other half of the year he is on the road chasing his passion for the outdoors: hunting, fishing, photography, and hiking.

@ericfisherphotography
ericfisherphotography.com

On a stormy evening in Alaska, I found myself lying in the sand photographing brown bears as they fished for salmon. I watched as a young male sprinted full speed through the water and did a superman dive in an attempt to catch a fleeting fish. The bear emerged from the chaos with a fish wiggling in its mouth. After it secured the fish in its massive teeth, the bear proceeded to walk directly towards me. When he was only 10 feet away he plopped down and devoured the fish in a matter of minutes. On my stomach I was able to capture the whole scene from a perfect angle.

02

FIRST RUNNER UP

WILDLIFE

JAMES HYDE — James Hyde is a guide, expedition diver, and photographer/videographer working above and below the water worldwide on the Lindblad Expeditions fleet. Living on Vashon Island in the Salish Sea he makes short films about the natural world to educate and inspire conservation. Hunting wild animals with a camera most of the year, he takes the fall to pursue black-tailed deer and elk.

@jamesfchyde
jameshydephoto.com

Flying fish are an open-ocean species that have nowhere to hide from predators. So when frightened, they burst from the sea and take to the air. An amazing adaptation, it is made all the more impressive knowing that water is 800 times denser than air and even the most advanced human technology struggles to succeed in both these mediums.

03

SECOND RUNNER UP

WILDLIFE

JEFF BRENNER — Jeff Brenner is a husband, dog dad, wildlife photographer and lover of the outdoors. After a series of life-changing events, Jeff turned photography from a hobby into a full-time career. His goal is to produce images that allow the viewer to connect to the subject in a way that fosters respect and appreciation. His hope is that his work can inspire others to get out and experience the diverse nature that reaches every corner of the US.

@jeff.n.brenner
jeffnbrenner.com

After coming across an undiscovered bald eagle nesting ground in California, I've made it a routine to visit these incredible birds of prey as often as possible. While I was observing this eagle intently survey the nearby river from its perch, it dove down toward the shallow water and grabbed a spawning kokanee salmon with its massive talons. Capturing this image was special to me, because it displays the eagle's focus and determination when on the hunt.

01

CATEGORY WINNER

WESTERN

AVERY SASS — Avery grew up in Nebraska with dreams to make a difference. Her family supported her and gave her the freedom to run after what made her feel alive. She hustled and tried new things and moved on from things she didn't like. Through her experiences in the American West, Avery learned about the kind of lifestyle that is restful, satisfying and impactful. She finds joy in documenting people in their natural element and learning about who they are and how they connect with the world. She connected immediately with documenting the West, as she learned how a ranch works, who true ranchers are and how they connect to land and animals. Avery currently works for a film-making company that specializes in humanitarian and documentary work.

@avery.sass
averysass3573.myportfolio.com

Silence and rain fall onto participants in the annual Hugo Ranch Rodeo, as the announcer's voice booms out a prayer. This was not the last time the cowboys and cowgirls were called to take their hats off for a respectful moment of silence that day, as bull and bronc rider alike rode with courage.

02

FIRST RUNNER UP

WESTERN

JOSEPH HAEBERLE — Joseph Haeberle is a photographer from Wyoming who chooses to celebrate the everyday beauty of our non-fiction lives. His work documents the American West and the characters within it. Joe currently lives in rural eastern Oregon with his girlfriend, dogs and horses.

@josephhaeberle
josephhaeberle.com

The picture is of the Lander, WY rodeo back in 2017 when I first started rodeoing myself. I was absolutely stoked on the sport and was at every rodeo I could find.

03

SECOND RUNNER UP

WESTERN

GARRETT MILANOVICH — Originally from Florida's east coast, Garrett Milanovich is now residing in Bellvue, CO on a small farm. He currently spends much of his time documenting Colorado's rodeo scene.

@garrett_milanovich
garrettmilanovich.com

Caitie Hefner racing across Wyoming.

01

CATEGORY WINNER

ART & ILLUSTRATION

MORGAN IRONS — Primarily a self taught painter, Morgan Irons began studying painting in 2015 following her move to a rural piece of land in Montana. It was there she began studying the work of master painters and has since sought out workshops with some of the top representational painters today. A figurative painter by nature, Irons believes in painting solely what she knows best, life on the land she lives. Her paintings are narrative and timeless in theme and palette. Morgan has been a featured artist in Fine Art Connoisseur's "Artists to Watch", Southwest Art Magazine's "21 Under 31: Young Artists to Watch in 2017", and Big Sky Journal's "Ones to Watch". She is a two-time recipient of the 2018 Elizabeth Greenshields Foundation Grant for emerging figurative painters. Irons is represented by Old Main Gallery in Bozeman, Montana where she currently lives and paints in a cabin on a mountaintop.

@morganirons
morganirons.com

"After the Storm" is a historical narrative based upon this essay by my great aunt, a longtime sheep rancher in Idaho: "We had avoided fire this time, but we had not made it through the night unscathed. Several hours later, Denny brought the grim news that fifty-one of our ewe lambs and two large bucks had been struck by lightning. We found the bodies on their sides, toppled by the force of nature, rigid yet huddled together still as they must have been when they were standing. It was a freak occurrence. They were not in a high place, or near trees, but in a green alfalfa field gathered for comfort against the bellicose summer storm. In this solace they shared death." Diane Peavey, Bitterbrush Country. I began this painting thinking about the archetype of the lamb, the reverent figure, and what we care for as stewards of the earth. Then the pandemic unfolded through Spring, this painting became an attempt to process that enormity.

02

FIRST RUNNER UP

ART & ILLUSTRATION

TEAL BLAKE — Teal was raised in Montana, on the eastern slope of the Rocky Mountains, surrounded by ranching country. Growing up in his father's studio, looking at C. M. Russell paintings and reading Will James books, it was hard not to pick up a pencil and start capturing his own visions of cowboys and the American West. Teal prefers to show what makes the traditional West: cowboys not always clean shaven; shirts not always creased; and their horses manes not always long.

@tealcokeblake
tealblake.com

"Blacks and Bays, Dapples and Grays" — oil painting 28"x40"
As a son of the "West," I wanted to portray the vastness and immense open country that I am drawn toward.

03

SECOND RUNNER UP

ART & ILLUSTRATION

SARAH NELSON — Sarah Nelson is an artist and illustrator in Los Angeles. Her work ranges from large scale pen and marker drawings to client and passion projects using the Adobe Suite and Adobe Fresco. In 2016, she started her own creative business, *Auslandish*, which later was renamed to WbySN (Works by Sarah Nelson). Through WbySN, Sarah creates commercial work for clients, collaborates with other creators, and runs her free illustrated resource: *This Amazing Planet*. She has had several solo exhibits around the country, nearly all have focused on environmental concerns and the overwhelming beauty of our natural world.

@sarah_ann_nelson
sarahnelson.art

"Brown Trout Finds Mouse in the Full Moon" — 20x16 Pen and Marker on Paper, 2020

01

CATEGORY WINNER

EMERGING

DAVID FASON — David Fason is an outdoor-focused editorial photographer based in North Carolina. He leverages his passion for fishing, wildlife and travel to create photos and videos that document his personal journeys. He is at home by the water and spends any time he can climbing along rocky creek beds or chasing waves on the coast. If paths cross, you will likely find him equipped with a fly rod and camera. When he is not on the search for indigenous fish, he is learning about local culture and cuisine. Photography allows him to share experiences and feelings with others when the stories of his travels are simply not enough.

@dafason
davefason.com

Hopkins, Belize local, Raydon, has a passion for learning everything he can about fly fishing. This shot captures his pure joy after we finished teaching him a couple fly patterns to practice during his dock light fishing. Fishing is not just a hobby in Hopkins, but a way of life.

LOON
Outdoors

02

FIRST RUNNER UP

EMERGING

CHRISTI HOLMES — Christi Holmes is a registered Maine hunting and fishing guide and enjoys all The Pine Tree State has to offer, from clam digging to beaver trapping to big and small game hunting with her Brittany spaniel. Christi founded the group Maine Women Hunters, a supportive community of over 2,500 women that builds confidence through guided hunts, ice fishing trips, skeet shooting lessons and social meet-ups.

@christiholmes

Due to their fish-eating diet, sea ducks taste fishy and are usually tossed in the coyote bait pile. I breasted out this hen eider and my Vietnamese friend, Oai, seared the meat and served her with his homemade ginger fish sauce. "Best to embrace the fish flavor," he said. He was right.

03

SECOND RUNNER UP

EMERGING

JARED BRUNO — Jared Bruno is a Pennsylvania state trooper and is the co-owner of the freelance media company Blueline Bowhunters, and founder and owner of J. Bruno Imagery. While he loves telling stories of his adventures in written form, his preference is to tell stories with his camera.

@jbrunoimagery
jbrunoimagery.com

This photo was taken during an Arkansas goose hunt and was the very first photo taken on the first morning. I stood in the field watching the decoys being laid out, wondering how I could capture this event in such foggy conditions all while keeping my camera functioning. It was then that the Polaris Ranger pulled in behind everyone to illuminate the field. The light from the Ranger gave me enough visibility to finesse the shutter and freeze the frame, but still allow movement of the people in the shot. This was one of those moments when you'd better have more luck on your side than anything else.

FAR AFIELD

Words by PAUL PETERSON
Photos by PAUL PETERSON & SAM AVERETT

PAUL PETERSON — SAM AVERETT

PRESENTED BY — **FIRST LITE**

After just two days in the field, we came down from the mountains of the Middle Fork country of central Idaho, with a gorgeous 175-plus-inch ram strapped to the back of my dear friend, hunting partner and roommate, Dan Breuer. He had filled his tag.

On our weighted descent, we bumped into a group of rafters. One of the gentlemen inquired about our purpose there. His name was Dave Baker, and while he was not a sheep hunter himself, he told us that his late grandfather had been — the prolific author and editor of *Sports Afield*, Jack O'Connor.

I was awestruck. I'd quoted Jack multiple times coming off the mountain on this day alone. Dave, the son of Caroline O'Connor, Jack O'Connor's daughter, took great pleasure in knowing we were familiar with Jack's work. That night, our groups shared a warm dinner and exchanged stories from our respective travels, agreeing to keep in touch.

It wasn't long before Dave reached out, sending photos of Jack Sr. and a note that read, *Good luck hunting — you guys embody everything good about hunting — patience, dedication, hard work and the willingness to get far afield!*

The compliment Dave paid us led me to reflect deeply on my own hunt in the Middle Fork country just a year prior. Patience, dedication, hard work and the willingness to go far afield are all qualities that were paramount to success on the greatest hunting adventure I've experienced to date.

For most of my life, sheep hunting didn't seem like an attainable goal given the rarity of tags and the cost associated with certain hunts. After establishing roots in Idaho and learning what hunting the Middle Fork entails, I committed to applying every spring. Luckily, I drew in just the second year.

The hunt for a Rocky Mountain Bighorn in Idaho can be considered a once-in-a-lifetime opportunity. If you're unsuccessful, the odds are not in your favor to return. If you do tag a ram, you can never harvest another Rocky Mountain Bighorn in the state of Idaho again.

The unit is not renowned for big rams and has a reputation of low success rates and being damn hard to hunt. I wanted to hunt sheep for the experience, not just to put a big head on the wall. This was my chance.

Drawing the tag was the easy part. The work began soon after celebrating, and being as resourceful as possible was my initial strategy. I called up biologists, former sheep guides and tag holders, as well as conservation officers and sheep-hunting enthusiasts. I ultimately decided to plan a long trip toward the end of the season. I committed to familiarizing myself with a species I'd never pursued, scouting and hunting more accessible portions of the unit until it came time to head in for the long haul. Four weekends were spent nearly rattling the frame on my old Chevy to bits on miles and miles of washboard road. Boot leather was shaved on steep, rocky terrain, and my back grew stronger under the continual weight of a heavy pack.

Time crept on and the days remaining in the season dwindled. All too quickly, the end of September had arrived and it was time to head in for the big rip, with my good friends and co-workers Nate Lijewski and Gregg Hedin along for the ride.

In late September, loaded with heavy packs full of food and gear to last no less than nine days, we boarded a nimble Cessna 206 and took off for some of the most rugged country in the Lower 48. Our confidence was high. We'd done our homework and everything we could to be successful up to this point. Now it was time to execute.

We were expecting weather. A front was moving in like a freight train, and the forecast called for a mild fall to quickly turn to winter. This proved true. Upon touching down next to the Middle Fork, we were greeted by 60-degree temperatures and bluebird skies. We shouldered our packs and began to move. Early on the trail, Nate and I parted ways with Gregg. He was to head along the river in order to keep an eye on the low country while Nate and I were headed up. By late afternoon, after climbing several thousand feet into the mountains, it began to spit rain, then sleet, then snow. Our efforts to glass were futile as dark clouds and fog engulfed the surrounding terrain. We were in our packable tipi by nightfall and quickly lit a fire in the titanium wood stove to warm up and dry our gear. We had no trouble quickly falling asleep to the sound of crackling wood and the pleasant warmth emanating from our shelter.

The next morning, I awoke to the walls of our tent hanging low over our heads as my breath showed clearly in the damp cold of our dwelling. I zipped open the door to see a fresh four inches of snow blanketing our surroundings. I pulled on cold, damp boots and clambered about the exterior of the shelter, scraping the fresh powder away in order to let the walls begin to breathe and dry. Nate built a fire in the predawn darkness. Weather was rolling everywhere as the sun rose. Our visibility was limited to a few hundred yards through thick fog, and it appeared the high country was completely socked in by low-hanging cloud cover. As we were unable to glass, and knowing it was in our best interest to conserve energy and play the long game, the day was more or less lost. We knew success depended on our ability to live on the mountain, whether it would take nine days or even longer. We weren't about to get antsy and burn ourselves out. We spent our time melting snow into potable water, sharing bad jokes and making fruitless attempts to get eyes on fresh terrain.

On day three, we woke to cold temps and favorable ceilings. As the sun illuminated the country, clouds began to slowly lift away from the surrounding peaks and steep hillsides. While the trip was still young and our patience strong, we broke camp and prepared to head for higher ground, eager to push ahead. The inclement weather had cost us valuable time to locate a ram, and the clock was ticking. After gaining a couple thousand feet of elevation we set to glassing from a pleasant saddle situated on a spine ridge. I sat behind my spotter and panned the hillside across from our position. Suddenly, the shape of something with a heartbeat came into view. In turn, my own heart skipped a step. I refocused the scope, and the bodies of four ungulates became visible. *They could be deer*, I thought, as I made sure not to bump my tripod and held stock still. As I peered intently through the lens of the spotter, with the only movement in the moment coming from my own pulse, the glass steadied and the curl of a horn came into focus. These weren't deer. They were rams. We'd found our quarry. What to this point had been a glorified camping trip was now a hunt.

It appeared there were at least two, if not three mature rams in the group, which consisted of four in total. They fed on the south slope of a steep, rocky face that was approximately 2.5 miles away on our line of sight. It was time to make tracks. With bags loaded down, we bailed off the spine ridge and began an arduous side-hill hike through slippery, snowy terrain. After hours of stumbling through, falling on and cursing the unstable ground beneath our feet, we finally arrived in a position 1,500 yards across a steep canyon from the rams. Nightfall was approaching quickly, and the steps that lay between us and them would not allow us to get in position for a shot that evening. We didn't expect them to move much and felt good about our chances of putting them to bed and finding them again tomorrow. The temperatures plummeted as the sun fell behind the mountain, and we watched the four rams until we could no longer see through our binoculars. With the last light gone from the sky, we retreated for the tent in order to warm our cold, tired bodies and to dry our damp and dirty gear.

We rose in the cold morning darkness and pulled on our insulating layers before returning to our glassing knob. Light snow fell as a gentle breeze swept the knob while we waited for the sky to illuminate our view. Almost as soon as our glass turned from a hazy gray to a crystal clear, we found them. They were bedded not 200 yards from where we'd last seen them the night before. But between us and the sheep lay a 1,600-foot drop and about a 1,700-foot climb up the other side in order to get even with their elevation. Not 15 minutes after getting eyes on the rams, heavy fog rolled down the mountain and we could hardly see more than 50 yards from where we stood. We wound up stuck in a cloud-encircled tent for the next five tedious hours.

As we anxiously struggled to pass the time, we reviewed video footage of the rams, naming them all. Tank was clearly the oldest and heaviest ram. His coat was a darker brown than the others, his belly hung low, and his horns were broomed back past his eyes. If we ever got a chance to make a move on him, and the wind was favorable, I felt confident in my 6.5 Creedmoor pushing a round out to 600 yards. Around noon, the weather began to break, and with unspeakable relief we confirmed the rams were still there. Almost instantly, Nate looked at me and asked, "You gonna make a move on these boys or what?"

"Sure am," I replied.

I headed back to the tipi and gathered my gear. There was a better than good chance Nate and I might end up separated, and I needed to be prepared to spend the night away from the tipi. My sleeping pad, sleeping bag and ultralight tarp were safely stowed in my pack. Nate and I had two-way radios and would be in touch periodically. I strapped on my rifle and headed into the canyon below; "Godspeed" was the last thing I heard as I began the stalk.

Over the next four hours, I would pick my way up the steep slope, the shifting gusts regularly causing me to pause. A snow squall accompanied by a west wind would pin me down against a cliff, as I was hesitant to move with the rams positioned to the east. Subsequently, strong thermals seemed to rip up from the bottom, giving reason to hesitate from pushing in too close. I constantly reminded myself not to rush up the hill. This was a long game. Even if the rams moved off, I could sleep on the slope and work to pick them back up tomorrow.

Around five o'clock, I reached the elevation and noted on the map that I was within 300 yards of the rams' last known position. With a steady thermal carrying up from the bottom, offering a crosswind, I belly-crawled to a cliff edge in order to peer across an avalanche chute. I was sure to quickly range several points on

I settled the crosshairs into his shoulder blade and slightly up toward his spine. He stood in a steep rockslide.

the opposing ridge, and all were at or just under 200 yards. I radioed Nate, but he couldn't see the sheep. Once again, the weather turned and snow flurries rolled through. The wind was still favorable, but visibility diminished to inside 100 yards. I did not move.

Lying there shivering, I was hopeful that if the weather broke, the rams may push toward me. After 20 minutes or so, it cleared briefly, and suddenly a ram popped out from behind the cliffs, 200 yards directly across the avalanche chute. Then another ram, and another. I quickly recognized the first ram to be Tank. My gun lay ready, but a branch obscured any shot opportunity, so I slid slowly to my right and settled in. I'd mounted my bipod in the fog and had my tarp handy to use as a rest under the butt of the rifle. Lying there prone and steady with the rams in clear view, it was a just a matter of deciding when to pull the trigger. Tank, the old ram, stood just a hair under 200 yards from the end of my barrell.

I settled the crosshairs into his shoulder blade and slightly up toward his spine. He stood in a steep rockslide. Putting a bullet through the high shoulder would anchor the old ram and prevent him from rolling potentially thousands of feet down the mountain. He grazed on curlleaf mountain mahogany, facing my position at a sharp quartering-to angle. As he shifted to continue feeding, his body was now more or less broadside. I picked a hair on the old ram's hide, thought about pulling the trigger, then breathed consciously and began to squeeze slowly, knowing I'd be surprised at the report of the rifle. The gun went off and the old ram fell dead, directly into the rocks below where he last stood. The other sheep bound away, and just as quickly as the explosion had rocked the mountainside, silence suddenly hung in the air.

It was done. We'd killed a mature ram in one of the most difficult units to hunt in the country. Patience, dedication, hard work and the willingness to get far afield had enabled us to harvest an incredible animal in one of the wildest places imaginable. I called Nate on the radio and relayed that we had a ram down and could hear a celebratory "Whoooooweee!" as he hollered through the clouds across the canyon. With just a couple hours of daylight remaining and the snow falling once again, I gathered my gear and moved over to the ram. Laying hands on the old sheep was a dream come true. His horns smelled of pitch and grass. His body steamed as snow began to cover his hide. I was in awe of his natural beauty, and for quite some time I sat next to him on the rocks, in the snow, with a hand on his horn, reflecting on what had just taken place.

I placed my phone on a nearby rock and took a photo on the self timer, snow falling incessantly. I knew the ram needed to be moved in order for me to break him down, so I carefully began to pull him across the steep rock slide toward a bigger boulder field where I could ensure he wouldn't slide away. Suddenly, I lost my balance and slipped on the wet rocks. As I fell onto my side, the ram's body lurched downward and began to pull me along with him.

Reason demanded that I let the ram go or risk a nasty slide myself. I finally released my grip on his horn. As I lay belly-down amid the rocks, I watched the ram flip end over end. I felt sick to my stomach, fearing he might be pummeled to bits falling down the mountainside. Somehow, after four or five full rotations, his body caught in a rock jam just before he would've vaulted over a cliff into the oblivion below. I picked my way down to him carefully. With the ram held in place by the rocks, I took a few minutes to move away some boulders near a cliff band and proceeded to dig away the soil to create a flat area in which the ram could lie and I could work on breaking down the meat and cape. The snow had briefly ceased, and I set up my good camera on a rock pile and snapped some quick photos. With weather beginning to roll in again, and daylight fading, I decided to set camp before working on the meat. There wasn't a flat spot in sight, so I climbed up to the nearest ridge and began kicking away rocks and dirt to create an area sizable enough to rest on. Finally satisfied with my excavation, I started pulling apart my pack to pitch my shelter. One problem — it wasn't in my bag.

Empty-handed, it hit me: I must've left it on the ground where I'd taken the shot. I needed to move, now. Quickly, I traversed back across the avalanche chute to retrieve my tarp. A couple fresh inches of snow had now fallen, and the tarp was nowhere to be found. A long search would cost valuable daylight and appeared ineffectual. I now had no shelter and would need to find another way to stay protected through the night. Attempting to get back to the tipi and stove with Nate would not be a safe or feasible option at this time of day, given the weather and adverse terrain. Traversing back to my now-useless flat spot, I wondered what to do and cursed myself for the mistake.

There wasn't much time to dwell on it. I began looking around for anything that could serve as cover from the impending weather and cold of the night. After bouncing up and down the mountainside looking about, I noticed a low-hanging doug fir situated on the precipice of a cliff. It was mostly dry beneath the tree, but the dry area was covered by boulders ranging in size from bowling balls to a 65-liter ice box. I got beneath the boughs of the old tree and began rolling away dirt and stone to create a space large enough for me to lie. I then broke boughs from the tree and situated them above the space between relocated boulders and onto an outstretched branch. This created a decent covering to stay the night. I would be protected from most forms of wind and snow, pending any true blizzard conditions. If things got too bad, I could wrap myself in my bag and all my layers while keeping a fire lit till morning.

Satisfied with my work, I returned to the ram at dusk, gutted him, and decided to let him lie through the night. Back at my new shelter as darkness set in, I savored a nip of whiskey from my lucky flask, then proceeded to build a fire and set to dry my saturated clothing. The variable snowfall and the toil of the day had left me soaked from precipitation and perspiration. For the next hour or so, I held my jacket and pants aloft near the fire. I wore wool next to my skin but wanted to be sure to have dry clothes to wear beneath my insulating layers in case the weather became more severe. Finally content with my drying operation, I grabbed my sleeping pad and bag to position in my crude lean-to. As I attempted to open the valve in order to inflate the pad, it tore at the edge like paper. An inch-and-a-half gash in the side of the pad was not repairable with my supplies. Lying in the dirt, I woke intermittently through the night, warmed by the feeling of satisfaction in handling the adversity of the day, and a successful harvest, thankful to only be experiencing light snow and mild wind.

The morning light brought wispy clouds breaking to blue sky. Upon crawling from the rocks, I quickly lit a fire and began to melt snow. Sitting with hot coffee in hand, I enjoyed the view looking across the snow-covered mountains back toward the Middle Fork. The country is beyond rugged and beautiful, highlighted by cliff and timber-strewn peaks jutting up 6,000 feet from the dry, golden-brown river bottom below.

I emptied my cup and gathered my gear, then made the short hike over to the ram and got to work. We would have heavy packs for the trip out; there was no way around it, and frankly, we wouldn't have wanted it any other way. I took care to debone the meat to save space and a bit of weight. We had a long hike ahead of us. Nate arrived just as I finished caping the head and horns. It was good to reunite, and we took a minute to share the stories from our perspectives on the events of yesterday and to briefly celebrate our success. With packs loaded down, weighing over 100 pounds a piece, we began what would be just over a 12-mile battle back to the river.

Over the course of the next two days, we slipped, stumbled, tripped, and rolled down snow-covered faces. We pushed, pulled and bushwhacked through willow-choked and avalanche-debris-strewn creek bottoms. It was the most physically demanding experience of our lives, and we relished it. We had killed a great ram deep in rough country, and we would get him back to the river whether it took two days or two weeks. Caught in terrain too dangerous to travel in the dark, we made camp halfway through the journey. By the evening of the second day we had made it back to the Middle Fork, and the hard part was over.

We'd spend the next couple of days waiting for a plane to be able to break through the still-inclement weather. The waiting didn't matter to us; we'd completed our mission and would later learn we were the only party to harvest a ram in the unit that season.

I have come to realize that the grueling hunts are truly my favorite hunts. Hunts that come with inherent challenges; hunts that instill some form of doubt in the most confident of outdoorsmen. Adventures that demand physical preparedness, mental tenacity and a degree of hunting prowess are usually attained by pulling a tag in areas known for rough country, low success rates, logistical boundaries and wary game. It is these types of hunts that inevitably lead to experiences worth talking about, experiences that teach as much mentally as they take physically. There is something beautiful that can stem from the suffering and hardship found there.

I return home with a greater appreciation for wild country and the wild animals I encounter, instilled with confidence in my ability to persevere through adverse circumstances. This hunt will leave a sweet feeling in my bones for a long time to come, an adventure of a lifetime which will be hard to beat, but I relish the miles of rugged country left to explore and the grueling hunts the years ahead may hold.

ARTIST FEATURE

NICHOLAS COLEMAN

Words by BILL RODEN *Photos by* TYLER SHARP

Western American Art has long defied categories and stylistic borders. Pioneering artists, shunned by traditional galleries, ripped assorted styles from classical works and artists. Yet these artists deviated from the usual subjects of delicate kings and queens or religious dogma; they were deemed rogues in their refusal to depict a natural world tamed by human hands. Many of the earlier artists in this genre applied impressionism, realism and expressionism to rougher motifs deemed unfit for white-gloved parlors and salons: rugged trail-breakers, fearless explorers, weary cowboys, wild game hunters, Native American warriors, contested ancestral lands and the ancient cultures who roamed their expansive landscapes. Western American art, throughout all its pivotal movements, guides the observer from a mere subject to a sense of wild places and wild people far outside of modern society.

Yet Western art continues its struggle to take its rightful place among mainstream audiences and the celebrated gallery walls long held hostage by curators and critics who evade both its artists and their work. For modern Western artist Nicholas Coleman, this culture clash serves as an appealing element that draws in an audience eager to trade modern life and art for wild landscapes. It's a source of inspiration that leads him to cast Western American Art with a wider lens. His work emboldens free-spirited imagination, while his cultural outreach encourages his followers to experience the West for themselves. This desire to push his audience to explore the raw landscapes in their own lives emanates from his core belief that those who cherish Western landscapes will, in turn, come to protect them. Nicholas Coleman is known for his efforts to increase access to America's wild places, but accessibility to art is a recurring theme in his approach to his clientele as well.

Nicholas Coleman's work emphasizes the key elements of a good story: scene, structure, event and plot. Every intentional brush stroke builds a story that evokes the common narrative of struggle, fortitude, and resiliency through both characters and the characterization. His romantic paintings inspire audiences to join his mission to preserve the fading heritage of the American West. Much of this is a result of his upbringing under his father, famed Western American artist Michael Coleman.

We recently spent time with Nicholas at his studio in Provo, Utah, to learn more about his work and the headwinds he embraces from critics and artists alike. We also discuss his successful use of social media to usher in a wider acceptance of Western artists and patrons by introducing new audiences to the people and culture of the West.

BILL RODEN — *Tell us a little bit about your background. How did you get into painting, and what does it mean to you?*

NICHOLAS COLEMAN — Growing up here in Provo, Utah, my father, Michael Coleman, was an artist as well. We would go do father-and-son type things. He'd take us fishing and hunting, and he even had a trap line here in Provo.

There used to be a golf course next to where we lived, so we were the muskrat trappers for the golf course — as a kid, that was great. Dad taught me how to skin a muskrat there. He also would give me a lot of books to read about the American West and buffalo and life and death in Yellowstone, and Barretech books. That was always magic to me, the history of the American West and the peoples that lived here and the early mountain men that came through this area.

EVERYBODY GETS SO USED TO BEING COMFORTABLE, AND THAT'S NOT HOW THE WORLD WORKS AND NOT HOW IT SHOULD BE WORKING. THERE'S SO MUCH OF THIS WORLD I HAVE YET TO SEE, AND I'VE SEEN A LOT OF IT, BUT I WANT TO SEE MORE.

When I came around, my dad would point out all the old places he used to go to and show me how they'd been ruined, but he also was looking constantly for new places to go. And that's how I was with my dad, just hunting, going out in the woods, and in our backyard, in the Wasatch Mountains, climbing the cliffs up behind my house.

Of all my siblings, I was the one that wanted to do those things the most, which hopefully made my dad happy. My mom probably got a little worried, with us heading up to Alaska and British Columbia to go moose hunting and things like that.

My dad went to Africa a lot, and I always thought he was going to be eaten by a crocodile or nailed by a buffalo or something, which from the stories I've heard, he came very close a few times. And I'm struck that he's still around at 74 years old, and not done. We talked about Teddy Roosevelt a lot and looked to him for just how life should be lived — not coddled and not comfortable by any means.

Everybody gets so used to being comfortable, and that's not how the world works and not how it should be working. There's so much of this world I have yet to see, and I've seen a lot of it, but I want to see more. And I'm constantly looking for new adventures and new experiences. I don't know if that'll ever die inside me.

By the time I was 21, I knew I wanted to be an artist like my dad. And I never thought it was easy, it's just one of those funny things that you enjoy, that you love and appreciate. And then you hope someone else is out there that has that same love and appreciation and is willing to pay you money to do it. But I count myself quite fortunate, and my father as well, to be doing this.

One of my mom's requests of me, when I was younger, was, "Okay, you finish college and then you can do whatever you want. If you want to be an artist, you can do that, but I want you to weigh your options and see what else is out there beside this." So I finished college within two years. Every semester I went, I thought, *I've got to get this. If I stop, I'll never go back because I hate this.*

I worked full-time in my dad's studio painting, and then I felt like I was going to school part-time, but still taking 15 credits here, 10 credits there. I was a busy guy, trying to get all the stuff done. I hated being on campus and trying to date.

I met my wife way back when, but we hooked up later in life when I ran into her again. I sat down with my parents when I was 21 and they said, "Okay. Now, are you sure this is what you want to do? This isn't an easy thing to do." And I said, "I never thought it

was. I can't imagine anything else I want to do. I've been mentally preparing myself since high school."

That's definitely how I got into it, just watching my dad. It's a lot of hard work. I got an apprenticeship under him without knowing that was what it was. I was just being his son, getting the paintings packaged, making sure they were getting photographed, driving things around, delivering things up at Jackson Hole.

I was just the errand boy, but then that transferred into, "Oh, I know how to do everything for myself now." My dad always joked about how he was the worst teacher because he was self-taught when it came to art. He went to college as well, but one of the professors took him aside and said, "You've got to get out of here. These guys are going to ruin you. They hate your guts."

So I just kept painting and working, and then some doors opened up.

BR — *Take us through some of the process of artistic growth. What were some of your earliest breakthroughs, and what do you feel are your current strengths?*

NC — Some of the earliest wildlife paintings that I loved to paint: birds, nests in their habitat, and life on the edge — hawks catching rabbits and squirrels. The interactions I saw spending time in the outdoors and in the boy scouts.

These are still current themes that I have in my paintings, man's eternal interaction with the natural world — less telephone poles and less parking lots and 7-Elevens. I think my enthusiasm early in my career, when I was a teenager and in my formative years, kept me pushing forward. I always had this confidence, but I think the hope for every artist is you're getting better with every single painting. And the more time you spend painting and the more time you spend observing, you're hopefully just absorbing all that information and energy that you can put back. I think enthusiasm for your subject goes a long way. I've talked to certain artists that said, "Should I start with a landscape?" I'm like, "Well, do you like the landscape?" "Oh, no. I hate the landscape. But you gotta start there."

And I say, "Don't do that. What do you love? Do that and do that better than anybody." And that's what my dad's advice to me was when I was deciding to be an artist. He asked, "What do you think about before you go to bed at night?" I said, "What I'm going to paint the next day." He's like, "Well, that's good. That's the answer I wanted to hear, because if there was anything else, I was going to say, 'Do that.'"

I'd put a moose in one of my paintings, and then it brings back all your funny memories for, say, a moose hunt, the fall smell, the dead, dying leaves. Or after you shoot the moose, there's a certain smell that you just never forget, and the hard work of quartering it to get it out. I think pulling the trigger is the easy part when it comes to hunting. And if you're a real hunter, you know that there's a lot more to it than just that. And I think that's what a lot of people fail to see when it comes to hunting and conservation. They think it's just a killing spree. And I've had a few social media things where people are like, "How could you?"

It was a painting of a hunter or a dead animal, and people freak out just about painting something like that, let alone a photograph. I've tried to be cautious navigating all that fun stuff just because I want to not have to worry about it. I try not to engage when it comes to idiots on social media. Facebook or Instagram.

And it's just not worth it and it just falls on deaf ears 99% of the time. There's always room for people who are actually researching and reading if they're interested in it. There's Carl Akeley, who was in charge of the Natural Museum in New York, the African wing. He was hunting with Teddy Roosevelt in Africa in the early 1900s, and he talked about how people only love the cuddly animals. In the early 20th century, they couldn't care less about the snakes and the frogs or the insects or that the whole natural world is one organism.

I know people get upset with the natural history museums, but they're showing the world and how much bigger the world was than just, say, New York or people's little towns and cities. And kids need the imagination. They need to see the natural world. And if you don't have an opportunity in these big cities, where else are you going to get it but these museums?

BR — *So it says your work has a somewhat editorial feel, as if you're imagining a world and capturing those romantic in-between moments that make the Western way of life otherworldly. Take us through your thought process on story and composition.*

NC — So, when it comes to my paintings, even when it comes to the bushes and sticks and twigs, the willows that, when you are a hunter, you climb through it and you weave your way in and out of it and have to scramble over it. You appreciate those kinds of things. And when you're looking at a painting, you think, "Hey, I have been there" — that's what I want to do. And I think it happens not on purpose, but it's just the way I like to tell a story.

BR — *You post on Instagram about the history of great Western artists who came before. Who were the key artists who influenced you the most, and in your opinion, which of these artists captured the true spirit of the American West the most?*

NC — I've tried to educate people on Instagram just because I love it. And it's like talking about Teddy Roosevelt or Carl Akeley, artists and certain figures that came and helped preserve the American West. Often with history, people look at it in a negative light. But the thing is it happens and you cannot erase it. And you need to preserve it, the good and the bad, and enjoy all aspects of it.

I do try to find the in-between moments, the back-in-camp moments or after they've skinned the animal and they're bringing it home. It's a way of life. I mean, it is life. The artist that I definitely look up to is the German-born artist, Carl Rungius, who spent a lot of time up in Montana and Canada and the Canadian Rockies hunting moose.

In a lot of his books, he has drawings of skinned animals. He did all these amazing studies and these etchings. So for wildlife historical artists, definitely Carl Rungius. And then those Western artists like Frank Tenney Johnson.

Certain cowboy artists: William R. Lewis and Thomas Moran, and Hans Von Bastad, another German guy that came through the 1880s. He's known for painting a lot of Yosemite landscapes in the Sierra Nevadas and places that help cement the American Western in the imagination of the whole world as a destination place that they needed to visit before they died. But a lot of my heroes, they're all dead.

BR — *Tell us a little bit about what a day in your life is like. More so, how are you living the world you've created, and how would you describe the current culture around what you're doing, the crossing-over lifestyle between hunting, Western art and motorcycle culture?*

NC — Growing up here in Provo, Utah was a nice bubble. My dad grew up loving the West and the Native Americans and the culture and then the way of life and hunting and growing up in the '50s and '60s in Utah. And all the stories I've heard, it's pretty magical.

I'm constantly hunting here in Utah, and fishing and fly fishing and traveling. I don't think a lot of people in Provo know what my dad has done or even myself.

I'm not too concerned about everybody knowing. I'm probably more known outside of Utah than in Utah, for whatever reason. For galleries, Montana has been great and Jackson Hole has been great; New Mexico has been good and New York of all places too has been pretty good over the years, and then recently in Texas. And as I've gotten older, my name's gotten out a little bit more. It's provided me with more means in order to do exactly what I want to do. And what's been fantastic about my particular work when it comes to hunting and wildlife is I'll meet like-minded people that will invite me to go on hunting trips, which makes it a lot more fun.

You saw my land cruiser with the tent on top. It's amazing to just grab the kids and head eight hours north and get out of town. And I want my kids to live the same way, because it's magic. Especially if it's miserable, they're really going to remember it.

BR — *So you've talked a little bit about how hunting plays into your work. But as a hunter yourself, knowing that your work crosses over between multiple genres, what are some of those themes you like to pursue around hunting?*

NC — I think when it comes to my paintings, it's just a reminder that it's out there still. I do like to make things timeless and just look at it and you go, "Yeah, that could be now or that could be 100 years ago." And I want to keep that. There is something about hunting that feels old-fashioned even though we're living in modern times, and I think some people think, "Oh, we're too civilized." The world is not civilized.

And it's one of those things for me, and I think my dad too, it's a compulsion. And part of it is just bringing our love of what we do to everybody else that loves it too and who's been out there as well. And it's always fantastic to meet like-minded people, and you share your stories. It's not even about bragging about anything, it's just sharing.

And my dad is the first guy to share. He never says no to anybody to come see his studio, because he just loves to share everything and loves the world and the natural world and all the fantastic things that are to see in it.

In July, my son did a ski camp. So we went to Mount Hood, and while he was at ski camp, we were doing hikes, and I was getting up early in the morning to go hike through this scary, creepy forest.

It was early in the morning, and I was looking at the giant volcano with Mount Hood right there and I'm like, "This is my first time. This is amazing. That's a volcano. That's a lake. There's a funny guy right there fishing with a spinning rod and there's a fire and there's blue smoke coming off the side."

And that just sparked a lot. I went through my photographs, looking through different color combinations. Every morning, my wife and I went back to the same spot, and while she was running, I was taking photographs and trying to look at different things. People were out canoeing, and they didn't know it, but they were all my models posing in different places. And there were some flying ducks swimming by and they'd come up thinking you're going to feed them, but they're being models. And they'll probably end up in a painting or two coming up here.

It's funny — just going outside, my brain just wakes up and people go, "What is wrong with you?"

And it's not so much like I'm containing enthusiasm. It's just, I love seeing it and I continue to love seeing it. And the sun will do so

many different things and cloud combinations of light early in the morning and then late at night when the sun's going down.

BR — *Tell us about your patrons, where you're selling your work and what the current state of the Western Art gallery world is. How do you navigate that?*

NC — I have a lot of repeat customers, thank goodness — clients that are like-minded people. And I have a few clients that I'm shocked about, like the president of Uline. This year, all the museum shows got closed down. A lot of galleries closed down for a few months. She was bummed out that she didn't even have the opportunity to buy any paintings, so she just reached out directly and got some fantastic deals.

This has been an interesting year in that people have just been reaching out: "Hey, what are you working on? Can I see anything? Do you have any moose paintings? Do you have any of this?" And I'll show them. So I've sold quite a few paintings.

People have been focusing on their homes and they want to bring things into their homes that make them feel better and happier. And I think my paintings are happy paintings for sure.

I think you constantly need to be open to learn and to grow and to be open to change, so when things happen, you're not stuck flat-footed and you can pivot and be better for it. I've had some life experiences where you're on a good path, then something smacks you in the face, devastating, and then you find yourself on a different path that's better, and more constructive. Because I think there is something truthful...and it's funny to talk about it like that, but truthful in the paintings. I've had people go, "Oh, it's romanticized." I say, "No, I've seen this." And they go, "Well, you'd never see a buffalo." And I say, "Yeah, you would. You'd see weirder stuff."

BR — *Tell us a little bit about the spirit of the West. How has it evolved, and where do you see it moving to creatively on the road ahead?*

NC — Every once in a while, I get worried about the spirit of the West just because people think it's more modern. They think it's changing or it doesn't exist anymore. A lot of it is a state of mind. It is a way of living. What's been great over the years is when I do find like-minded people, I find out how many more there are people who are moving into more open spaces.

People would always talk about how terrible people are for the environment. The only people that give any validity to the environment are humans. Like, "If you get rid of humans, the earth could heal and it would be better." Well, who would honor it? Who would say, "This is special or unique?" Nobody. It'd be an empty planet devoid of anybody that says, "This is amazing."

And art can be just about whatever you want it to be. I definitely tried to bring it back to something that could actually happen and still, in my opinion, is magic. When *The Revenant* was coming out, I know the guy — he just lives up the road in Heber — who trained Bart the bear.

While I was talking to him, he was like, "Oh, yeah. They're doing the show about the Revenant and they're going to use my grizzly bears to do the movie." And then I talked to him a few months later, and he said, "Well, they wanted the scarier bear, so they went digital." I'm like, "Scarier? How can you get scarier than a real grizzly bear?" He said, "I don't know. They wanted that."

EVERY ONCE IN A WHILE, I GET WORRIED ABOUT THE SPIRIT OF THE WEST JUST BECAUSE PEOPLE THINK IT'S MORE MODERN. THEY THINK IT'S CHANGING OR IT DOESN'T EXIST ANYMORE. A LOT OF IT IS A STATE OF MIND. IT IS A WAY OF LIVING.

BILL RODEN — TYLER SHARP

BR — *Western art is often branded as whitewashing or racist. How would you respond to someone who doesn't believe your work on Native Americans is authentic?*

NC — So this is interesting. Recently, someone said, "How do you not get any criticism?" Because I really haven't had any, which is almost shocking in this day and age to not have it.

For the last probably 20 years or so, we've been working with a foundation called American Indian Services, and they provide scholarships for Native Americans in the West. They're set up all the way to college, all the way to where they get jobs. So I mean, if they stay in the program, it's not just a, "Here's a scholarship, good luck." They work with the students all the way through.

So I've worked with some amazing people and I'm happy to donate paintings for fundraisers, because I want culture to live on. And the history of the American West is fraught with terrible stories of genocide and mistreatment.

I remember reading *Blood and Thunder*, where Kiowa or Apache Indians would take Irish and Scottish children as captives. But when they went to their rescue, they didn't want to go back. And I always thought I would be probably one of those kids who wouldn't want to go back to that way of life. The Native American way of life was often nomadic, and I have a feeling their existence was amazing and fantastic. Even when I was a little kid, I always wanted to grow up to be a Native American.

BR — *Not to answer your question for you, but the fact that you have respect and that it seems like your intentions with the work are pure in that sense — because you do have respect — and that you want to continue that, it comes through in the work. It's sincere.*

NC — Over the years, I've realized I'm not trying to get in anyone's face. I'll paint what I paint. I know who I am. I think that's a big part of it and what I'm doing. My purpose isn't that. But my purpose actually is to be constructive and helpful.

BR — *Fine art is expensive and, oftentimes, reserved for the wealthy. In an era that aims to remove barriers in all corners of culture, how do you address the cost of art in the gallery world that hasn't evolved much in terms of access and affordability?*

NC — So lately, the last few years, I've thought the exact same thing, about accessibility, because I really do want artwork in the hands of anybody. And a lot of times, it might not make business sense. If someone's excited about something, I'm totally willing to give them a great deal. And sometimes, I've lost money on certain deals, but I like the person so much because they're so excited about it.

BR — *What's the biggest regret you have creatively, or what's the one thing you feel that you've yet to create or accomplish?*

NC — Hopefully, there aren't too many regrets, but what's funny is I'll visit museums around the world and I'll see artwork created by certain artists. And I'm in awe sometimes.

There's a Waterhouse painting of the Judgment of Herod and there's John the Baptist's head on a plate and the painting is ten or eleven feet high and six feet wide. And I'm looking at this thing going, "What am I doing?" Granted, I don't paint religious scenes. It was one of the most amazing paintings I've ever seen in person. And I thought, "Wow, I gotta try harder." And so hopefully, my regrets turned into me working harder and putting in a little more thought, effort, energy going forward.

FACING PAGE — Nicholas in the studio of his father and artistic mentor, Michael Coleman. They live just a few blocks away from eachother in Provo, Utah, which makes creative collaboration and the exchange of inspiring tales of adventure that much easier.

BR — *You mentioned this earlier about your dad asking what you thought about before you go to bed. But what would you do if you couldn't paint anymore?*

NC — I've thought about it too over the years. I'm like, "What else do I like to do?" I like to eat. I think I would be pulled back to art somehow, and it would be always coming back to painting. I'm like, "Oh, maybe I'll work for a gallery, granted I hate people." That's terrible to say. But I hate the idea of having to be a salesman or sell.

I hate talking about myself when it comes to, "Hey, look, all my paintings are great or this and this," because I know certain artists that are just fantastic at selling themselves. I'm hoping my work can speak for itself and so I don't have to. That's my whole goal.

And when my wife comes with me to shows, she's great because she's better-looking than I am, friendlier than I am. And she does a great job selling my work or talking to people, and again, engaging with people.

BR — *Are there other things that if you could expand outside of the current genre of gallery or collectors, what would be some things you want to do?*

NC — Now that I'm getting older, I've had a lot of younger artists come to the studio, and they'll bring me some of their artwork to look at, to give them pointers and tell them how to get to galleries. And I always say, "Well, don't ever think that you've made it because you're in a gallery."

There's a thing in Utah called Creative Collaborative, where you discuss and talk about your work and people ask you questions about how you do certain things or how you go about certain things. People are in all different kinds of creative fields, and some overlap, which that's the hope, that you're helping certain people that are struggling in a certain aspect to solve a few problems.

And then over the years, my dad's been the greatest example of, like I said, sharing...

BR — *How do you want to be remembered?*

NC — I think any honors of men are transitory. I think I'd like to be remembered, hopefully, as just someone who shares their passion and enthusiasm and the love of the outdoors. And it happened to be with artwork. I think that might be the way to be remembered, and I thought, *"Man, I'm not sure how much future we have left going forward, but I doubt I'll make it in any of our history books or even a footnote."* And I don't think that's the goal. But it sure would be nice to be in a book of some kind.

BILL RODEN — TYLER SHARP

Laura Zerra is a survivalist and hunter who currently calls Montana home. She has spent her entire adult life honing her craft in every major ecosystem on the planet, and used her expertise to survive for a combined total of 156 days on the Discovery show Naked and Afraid. *Driven by a desire to interact with the wilderness in a real way, she is constantly seeking experiences to push her edges and learn new skills.*

LAURA ZERRA

LAURA ZERRA —TYLER SHARP

Words by LAURA ZERRA *Photos by* TYLER SHARP

EARNING OUR STORIES

The rain was relentless, mixed indistinguishably with my sweat. The last streaks of daylight faded as darkness descended, and I felt the icy coldness of the night seep in. I was on a month-long, solo antler hunting trip in the mountains of Idaho, and I had walked thirty miles with a pack nearly the equivalent of my own body weight. Exhausted and soaking wet, I knew that if I didn't find a way to warm up soon, I would be in trouble. The narrow path I was on had a steep drop to a river on one side, and a cliff on the other. There was no viable option to stop and start a fire or crawl into my sleeping bag, so I pushed on.

Every muscle in my body was screaming, but it was my feet that commanded attention. Several large, pillowy blisters had formed, and gradually expanded to include every toe and even the soles of my feet. These filled, burst and ripped through layer after layer of skin, all of which now dangled limply like wet tissue paper. Several of my toenails were barely hanging on, having been pushed to almost a right angle by blood-filled pockets. I gritted my teeth and peeled them off. The heavy weight I was carrying had expanded my feet laterally, the compression of my boots compounding the excruciating pain. I could feel my heartbeat in my wounds. I took them off and pushed forward. The patchy snow on the trail numbed the raw flesh of my bare feet, offering a brief reprieve in a trail of bloody footprints.

Every fiber of my being was yelling for me to give up, but I convinced myself to take just ten more steps, and then ten more, for what seemed like an eternity. I knew something my body didn't — I couldn't stop. There was no one there to save me, and no room to feel sorry for myself. It didn't matter what I thought or felt about the situation at that moment. I was in it, and there was only one way out. So I did what I had to do. I kept going.

Resilience is more than a word to me; it is the collective drive behind experiences like this and countless more, all uniquely different and yet somehow the same. They stand alone, distinct, yet they are all colored in the same hue. They have become etched, irrevocably, on my bones.

When I think of resilience, I remember some of the darkest times in my life. I remember when the pain became a character so real that I could almost see his face; his voice echoing in my head, telling me there was no way I could keep going and that I had to give up. I remember my own self-doubt, and fleeting thoughts of whether I'd finally pushed too far, how I could have done things differently, if it even mattered anymore or if it was too late.

I don't seek out these experiences because I enjoy pain, or because I want to die; rather, it is because I want to live. These are moments I hold closest to my heart, that have significance and value beyond any time of comfort I can recall. After the dust settles, I feel profoundly alive, and I know what it means to embrace my humanity. It's simultaneously empowering and humbling. It has made me aware of the fact that I'm not different or special, and that like all of us, I'm subject to the same forces that have affected countless generations before me. In this way, we are deeply connected to our ancestors, who survived because of their ability to be resilient; to face the unforeseen and sometimes unimaginable, to meet it head on, and to push through despite all odds.

Resilience is part of our collective story. It is innate for all of us. We are capable of so much more than we know, and it is in these defining moments of hardship that we have the opportunity to uncover our own strength. Though often dormant in our lives of routine and imagined safety, this latent hardiness is always there, hidden, just waiting to be unlocked.

The raw reality of life is displayed with a stark honesty in the wild, and I'm grateful for the lessons that it has taught me. I've learned that our power lies not in our ability to control the uncontrollable, but in how we respond to these situations. Our power comes from focusing not on what you don't have or what you wish you had, but on what is around you and how you can use it. We can revel in the opportunity to control our reactions instead of feeling like victims of circumstance.

Regardless if we are on a mountaintop in the wilderness or in the heart of civilization, uncertainty is inevitable. This thought can be harrowing for some, but there is so much hope if you know where to look.

It becomes a choice between letting our greatest trials defeat us, or letting them become our greatest teachers. Confidence in our ability to be resilient is what allows us to overcome our fear of discomfort, to live fully, to never give anything less than everything, and to truly earn our stories.

And I promise you, it is always worth it.

LAURA ZERRA —TYLER SHARP

RED DESERT

Words by JONNAH PERKINS *Photos by* CHRIS DOUGLAS

On the face of it, fattening up cattle on grass in the Red Desert of southern Wyoming looks like squeezing nectar from dried wildflowers — possible, though unlikely. But if you take one square yard of the sagebrush steppe and really stop to look, you'll find forage that has been supporting megafauna for millennia. Wildland shrubs create a canopy that fosters a mosaic of lichen. Each color marks the bedrock of varied geology on which this steppe has grown. The texture of this landscape cannot be described in words but instead a feeling. There is a starkness in this landscape, found more in what is not there than what is. If it weren't for the intermittent buzz of dirt bikes, it would be hard to place this time in history.

RANGE–LAND

Mark Carter grew up in the cowboy country of the Red Desert, as a third-generation son of a rancher. If you ask Mark to tell you what's hard about a cattleman's life, he gives a youthful but weathered grimace. "We grew up gnarly, around livestock and motorcycles, and horses bucking us off. My dad wasn't like, 'How are your feelings today?' He just said, 'This is what we're doing. The nights may be yours, but the days are mine.' That's what he always told us."

The ranching life is woven into the Americana fabric that defines the West, but cowboys are a dying breed. The consolidation of the beef industry has cornered many producers into a system of feedlot operations driven by commodity rates that are at the whim of global markets. For the ranchers that make up the Ten Sleep, Wyoming-based Carter Country Meats, leaning into the headwind has become a stubborn mission, if not a way of life. Between the three Carter men — Richard, Mark's father and his older brother, RC — cracking the commodity puzzle has lit a fire so bright that it's hard not to be drawn in.

To understand the origin of the cowboy, we first need to recognize the role of predators, like coyotes, wolves and cougars, that managed these grasslands before human intervention. Their presence pushed large ruminants across the landscape and created movement that the herd would not have made on their own. The Red Desert holds the largest unfenced area in the continental United States, providing open range for the greatest pronghorn migration south of the Canadian border. Mark sees the role he plays as an agent of environmental pressure on their cattle as part of the flow of the grassland ecosystem. "It's natural for animals to be on this land, it's healthy, and it's just as natural for us to be behind them, chasing them."

The drier the environment, the greater acreage a rancher needs to graze their livestock. The Carters both own and rent rangeland across Wyoming. On a Bureau of Land Management (BLM) lease that augments the family's home ranch four hours to the north, Mark and RC push a herd of cow-calf pairs through Bull Springs, a perennial water source that bisects the Continental Divide. Though this natural spring sits at just under 7,000 feet above sea level, the water that percolates up from the bedrock will never flow off toward the Atlantic or the Pacific oceans. The Continental Divide Basin holds groundwater and melted snowpack in place, supporting forages like salt sage, Indian rice grass, squirrel tail and grey horsebrush for the Carter Country Meats Angus beef herd. In an agricultural climate where the pressure of continually ratcheting up productivity is commonplace, RC stands behind his need to adapt the herd size to the status of the forage from year to year. "The stocking densities here in this country are a lot lighter than up in Ten Sleep just because it's really sandy soil, so it doesn't hold as much moisture. But on this lease, which is about 340 square miles, I think there's probably 2,000 animals on it, depending on the year. On good years, when it rains, the forage would maintain even more than that."

Desertification of land is hard to reverse in high desert ecosystems. The Carter sons learned early on from their father that it's the job of the rancher to be a steward of rangeland balance. In the vastness of the Red Desert, BLM land is surveyed using lines on a map, not necessarily accounting for natural features that influence the viability of individual pastures. But the value of securing a lease and becoming a student of the terrain is not only smart business for the rancher, but an act of conservation in the greater picture of regenerative outcomes. Understanding what areas are most sensitive to erosion and where animals can access water requires an intimate sensitivity of the rancher with his rangeland. Mark points to several areas across the horizon. "All these wells are solar wells. My dad put these in when he first got this lease, so he has water all over."

TO UNDERSTAND THE ORIGIN OF THE COWBOY, WE FIRST NEED TO RECOGNIZE THE ROLE OF PREDATORS, LIKE COYOTES, WOLVES AND COUGARS, THAT MANAGED THESE GRASSLANDS BEFORE HUMAN INTERVENTION.

Richard's commitment to developing the desert pasture took an investment in time that unfolds much more slowly than grazing systems in regions with more precipitation. RC points out that many BLM programs are not nuanced enough to account for individual microclimates, but it all comes down to relationships. "You got to have the right BLM agent who is eager enough to look outside the box a little bit. We are working on some stuff with our range gal right now to go in and redo all the fences based off of topography. We look where the water's at, the soil quality, and where we've got a bunch of canyons, rather than build a fence where it doesn't make sense."

Weathering the sand, rock and desert scrub on horseback is a longstanding tradition of the cowboy life, but Richard Carter realized decades ago that he could cover far more ground on a dirt bike. Mark remembers how his father put innovation in front of folk rituals to get the job done. "We grew up on horses. It was the standard-issue Western way. Dad, he's still all about the horses, but just out of functionality, for being short-handed in big country with lots of cattle, that's when we added motorbikes into the mix. I think the first time I ever chased cows on a motorcycle I was in the fifth grade. You can put in 100 miles a day on a bike. You just can't do that on a horse." Ripping through the desert on a motorbike may seem at odds with cowboy culture, but innovation is what has allowed Carter Country Meats to thrive with a nimble team. Richard's roundup strategy now utilizes dirt bikes for their speed and efficiency in covering rough terrain while horses still offer the holistic proximity needed to be close to the herd as it moves across the range. RC's wife, Annia, and their three sons, are all skilled cowboys and play a vital role in the ranch operations.

Mark's scrappy childhood, driving cattle and running a ranch alongside his dad and brother, created a hardened approach in other areas of his life. Many people know Mark more for his career as a pro snowboarder than for the work he does pushing big animals through the high desert. "I'm a rancher in the summer and then I'm a snowboarder in the winter. It's all just navigating the natural environment and it's very intuitive for me to just be outside all day. This is what I've been doing my whole life. I didn't have the best snowboarding gear growing up, and I'm used to being cold on a horse, but that was good because then I just learn how to tough it out. There's no bad weather, just weak people."

The worlds of adventure sports and food production seem to be at opposite ends of the spectrum, but living his split life has made Mark stronger in both disciplines. "There's a lot of overlap. With ranching, we were just taught that there's no quitting. You just got to find a solution no matter what the job is. Then, in snowboarding, I take that same mentality into it. I'm a glutton for punishment; I don't mind suffering one bit." Mark started his snowboarding career later than most kids making a life out of the sport, but he quickly moved up the ranks to land coveted top-tier sponsorships. Now, he travels the world in between grazing seasons. "They're different careers, but I would say being a snowboarder is a lot easier than being a rancher because I get to choose to go out on the days that I want, and it's tough, it can be dangerous, but I know what the

WEATHERING THE SAND, ROCK AND DESERT SCRUB ON HORSEBACK IS A LONGSTANDING TRADITION OF THE COWBOY LIFE, BUT RICHARD CARTER REALIZED DECADES AGO THAT HE COULD COVER FAR MORE GROUND ON A DIRT BIKE.

ranchers are doing, and I think, 'this ain't that hard.'"

Growing beef and selling beef are two different things. The Carters have worked for years to stay in the regional supply chain. Buying into the grass-fed ideal comes at a high cost, though. Restaurants and grocery stores don't usually align their money with their projected values, outwardly aligning with local food sourcing, but not usually showing up for small-scale producers. RC knows that competing against volume producers is an uphill battle. "Everybody wants to stay local and grass-fed and feel good about themselves, but as soon as it comes to the money, they buy the cheap stuff. The whole system starts with corn and the big processing plants. It's damn-near impossible to even compete with them." In the current commodity landscape that incentivizes conventional corn production through taxpayer subsidies, more and more acres of farmland are being pulled into a monocropping system. Livestock feed has become a strategic link in the corn surplus that ultimately benefits seed-biocide monopolies, while extracting from the land and compromising the health of the humans and animals it feeds. But pushing into a market that is stacked against them has given the Carters even more determination.

The brothers caught a break when they connected with a restaurant group that was drawn to their modern cowboy story. RC brought two cows into the sales meeting, and the product spoke for itself. "They said, 'We love it. How do we get more of this?'" RC recounted. "So we bought 80 cows from my dad and one of those overseas shipping containers for storage. We killed 80 cows and the restaurant guys are like, 'We'll take two a week.' I'm like damn, finally, a home run, but then they only bought one cow a month. I was like, 'We are in so much shit'. Because it's worse than having a banker, when you borrow money from your dad. Every time he comes over, he's like, 'Hey, you got that money?'"

In March 2020, to reduce reliance on the grocers and restaurant accounts, Mark and RC launched a direct-to-consumer beef distribution program under the family ranch brand, Carter Country Meats. With the global beef machine creating an increasingly complex web of international trade, the Carters have put their stake in keeping their products as close to the source as possible. Mark feels that the ranchers who manage the animals and invest in the environmental viability of the land should hold the value of the product. "It's just unfortunate that the ranchers, the guys that carry the animals their whole life, don't get paid shit and the guys that hold onto it for two weeks get most of the money. We can all agree that nobody wants to see huge feedlots stuffed full of unhealthy animals, but then you come to places like this where you see these animals live better than most people. They get to live out here and just eat grass for their whole lives. That sounds pretty cool to me."

RC sees that the system is stacked against his family's ranch, but the solution, he says, lies in working outside of the system. "From the grass to the soil to the cows and then to the beef, the whole thing is not set up for a small rancher. The wholesale industry convinces the consumer what foods should cost, and for ranchers like us, we just can't meet that." RC and Mark see a path around the global wholesale marketplace through their direct relationships with their customers. RC's vision is to take grass-fed beef out of the premium product category. "I don't want to sell it to the 1%; everybody should be able to afford good food."

The bottleneck for the independent beef producer ultimately lies in the processing. Over the years, the commodity beef market has elbowed artisanal butchers out of rural communities, leaving small-scale ranchers with little choice for processing. RC explains: "It costs us a thousand dollars just to have them processed, but if I can do that on my ranch, then we can avoid sending them 500 miles to the closest processor, and then shipping that back. I have a skilled butcher that can add a couple hundred bucks to the quality of my meat. We can out-compete those guys, but it has to happen on a local level. Local is where it's at."

What Mark and RC are creating is a vertically integrated model that will bring back ranching traditions that have been reduced to relics of the West. Mark doesn't want to romanticize the ranch life he was born into. "I don't really care if people think I'm a cowboy or not. I just do the job and help my dad with what he needs. When it comes down to it, I don't know more of a cowboy than him because he can do everything. You're like a multi-tool, being able to get the job done. That's a rancher." The Carters' commitment to conserving the Red Desert grassland ecosystem and rebuilding rural food systems is forged in a steadfast belief that traditional ranching is still a viable path. While raising and selling beef is stacked against the independent rancher, the Carter family is taking a traditional way of life and forging it into their own vision. Through their grit and tenacity, they have created a new frontier that returns to a way of life that existed before the business of beef was removed from the hands of the rancher.

This is the first in a series of stories about the Carter family. Modern Huntsman will be exploring the family's evolving regenerative beef cattle production and their textured history on the Wyoming landscape, among other things.

WHAT MARK AND RC ARE CREATING IS A VERTICALLY INTEGRATED MODEL THAT WILL BRING BACK RANCHING TRADITIONS THAT HAVE BEEN REDUCED TO RELICS OF THE WEST.

THE STRANGEST OF PLACES

Story by LAUREN OWENS LAMBERT

The never-ending hum of passing cars is the kind of sound you notice only in its absence. As I follow Don through the thick understory of pricker-bushes and poison ivy, typical of a secondary forest in New England, I think to myself, "You can't really escape the crowdedness of this place." There is always the noise of rumbling motors, the beeping of trucks and the barking of neighborhood dogs. "There are no leaf blowers in Idaho," he says. "But here, there is a small window of time, when the light is a soft gray, the air is crisp and birds are not yet awake where you find the stillness and quiet of nature. That's why I do it." In these small patches of woods between homes, beside highways and through property lines are deer — lots of deer — and the people who hunt them.

Don Merry, a bowhunter from Duxbury, a town in the South Shore of Massachusetts, drives up a winding gravel driveway to a large, white colonial home. He steps out of the truck and sprays a scent-concealer onto the soles of his shoes before walking over to greet the homeowner, Katina Manning. "You mind if I scout out some spots for the stand and set up a camera?" he asks. Don Merry has 10 stands on eight different public properties and backyards throughout the town of Duxbury, and has been hunting Katina's property for the past six years. Open communication and even friendship with a wide range of property owners is key to hunting in these suburban woods.

"You are always welcome," shouts back Katina. They spend the next 20 minutes catching up about family, summer fun, work and, of course, hunting.

An archer can legally hunt as long as they are at least 150 feet away from any public road or highway and 500 feet from a residential home, or have explicit permission from a homeowner to hunt within that 500-foot limit. Navigating the regulations of where an archer can hunt in these suburban environments is tricky. The rules change with the type of land and vary from town to town. Colin Dowd, an archer from Marshfield who was introduced to suburban hunting in the area by Don, says that you cannot hunt in any town-owned conservation land in Marshfield, but you can in Duxbury, which is the next town over. In some cases there are non-hunting zones within a swath of legally huntable forest, depending on what it abuts, such as a campsite. But when it comes to being a private landowner, "If you don't post your property and it meets the criteria, then it's huntable. So, basically, you can go anywhere in the state with the exception of some conservation lands," says Don. In recent years, Don has advocated for himself by going in front of the town's conservation commission to petition to hunt on carefully selected areas of conservation land and has won every time. Lots of dedication is spent learning the law, advocating for the safe hunt, and building relationships with community members in order to hunt comfortably in this human-infused environment. "It takes a lot of research to hunt here, but once you figure it out, it's all worth it," says Don.

Dave Cederlund, a bowhunter from Hingham, has had a relationship with Anne and Charlie Gregory in Duxbury for 20 years and has been hunting their 10 acres for most of that time. "Dave always gets something," says Anne as she hands him a gift of homemade bread and butter pickles in appreciation.

Massachusetts is the third-most densely populated state in the country next to Rhode Island and New Jersey, with approximately 6.8 million people squeezed into 10,565 square miles. The deer population in the same area is estimated at 100,000 by state Fish and Wildlife, and the suburban deer like to stick close to the houses. They feel safer next to the homes, where there seems to be no threat, but when they smell humans off the beaten path they instantly become wary. An urban bowhunter is not only navigating the usual hunting challenges, such as learning territory ranges, behavior, biology and tracking techniques, but also a world of tight regulation and taboo.

To be a successful bowhunter in suburbia, one has to be respectful, transparent and understanding of peoples' discomfort with hunting. It takes time to build healthy relationships with the community and to gain the trust of a property owner. Don says that it's all about respect. "I would love to just dress the deer on site and dump 100 pounds of guts before the drag, but we can't always do that. What if a dog gets into it? Or a person stumbles upon it during a walk?" That kind of behavior would make hunting look bad. A big difference between hunting coastal Massachusetts versus wild open spaces is the culture. "Coming out of the woods dressed in camo with a bow or a gun here, you will get looks," says Don. "But in Idaho or places like that you'll get a nod and a 'How'd ya do?'" Fighting any stereotype is a challenge, but Don, Colin, Dave and the others like them seem to be representing the best side of hunting.

Bowhunting between homes in the Bay State is a new tradition in the making. Hunting Plymouth county in this way started to gain traction sometime in the early '80s, according to local hunters, with towns such as Andover opening up hunting opportunities as recently as 2010. Don Merry says that "if you were to ask an old-timer right now, they would never think of hunting these woods. They would make their annual trips up to Maine, Vermont or New Hampshire to hunt." He continues, "Now my son and his friends are getting into it and some of my younger co-workers, like Colin, are also into it now. Sure, I have lost some spots," he says with a chuckle, "but it's great to see the younger generation picking it up."

While there is a slight downward trend in hunting across the nation, here in the Northeast, regulations seem to be loosening, opening up new or historically huntable areas. In 2015, deer hunting was made available in the Blue Hills State Reservation for the first time in a century, and is the closest place to Boston where hunting is allowed. Zone 11, Plymouth County, which is home to around 520,000 people, was the most productive zone in the state 2018, and there are active public hearings to extend the archery season.

Dave Cederlund says, "I never considered hunting Massachussets. But then I saw all of these deer and thought, 'Why am I hunting in areas with a lower deer density?' My success here per hour in the stand is way better than in Vermont and Maine."

Hunting these fragmented sections of woods close to home is an effective way to manage the inflated deer population, provide local meat and connect with nature. "Because they don't have as much space here, it's much easier to pattern the deer in the suburbs," says Dave. Over time, native predators have been eradicated, such as cougars and wolves, and humans have fragmented the lands, thus disrupting the food chain. This has led to an overpopulation of deer; when populations get too high, they increase the threat of tick-borne illnesses and impact the understory of a forest. With larger trees blocking out sunlight, they can eat away at habitat for smaller animals such as chipmunks, rabbits, birds, racoons and foxes, to name a few. Don says that conservation groups all over the country are letting hunting take place for that reason.

The whir of commuting cars and the distant sound of children playing start to fade away with the falling of the sun as the archers relax into position among the tight strips of forest outlining soccer fields, horse farms and homes — there they wait. "I bow hunt for whitetails because I feel a huge connection to them, to nature and the food that they offer," says Don. With a deep appreciation for the wild, for the animals and the community of people who open up their yards, urban and suburban archers discover that the hunt will take them to the strangest of places.

LAUREN OWENS LAMBERT

CHEF FEATURE

SARAH GLOVER

Words by KATIE MARCHETTI *Photos by* STEFAN HAWORTH

STEFAN HAWORTH

The ambient noise of waves crashing and birds singing their approval breaks over the line first. Sarah Glover is checking the surf report when she answers my call from half a world away. Her Australian accent and easy, joyful laugh place her perfectly on the sunny coast of Tasmania, where she was born and raised and resides again today. A childhood of island exploration, and tea breaks to play in the kitchen, led her to culinary school at 16. An education in traditional French cuisine took her on a laborious path where the mile markers included her own restaurant in NYC, and a bakery in Bondi Beach, before she returned home to find that the recipe for her own life was waiting in the bushland of 'Tassie.'

For Chef Glover, the missing ingredients were always fresh air and an open flame. Today, she takes people outside and off-grid with her catering business, Wild Kitchen. Armed with a knife, and a few basic tools of the trade, Sarah teaches workshops for adults and children alike, where she encourages people to use local ingredients from the farm, field and sea in their quest for self-sufficiency.

The author of the Wild Adventure Cookbook *shares her thoughts on ingredient sourcing, wild game cooking, international food traditions, recipes for fresh kangaroo, and what she isn't rogue enough to try.*

KATIE MARCHETTI — *Why don't you tell me a little bit about your upbringing? What was family life like, and how did you discover your love of cooking?*

SARAH GLOVER — I grew up in Tasmania, or Tassie for slang. Australians like to abbreviate — we shorten everything we can! My parents had my two older brothers and me, and then they actually had an eight-year gap and then had five more; so I'm one of eight kids, with five brothers and two sisters. My parents decided to homeschool us, which wasn't really a trendy thing to do back then. We had this amazing house that was on the water, and there was a bit of a bushland in front of us. My brothers and I were always really adventurous. We loved being outdoors, and would try and do school as quickly as we could so we could run out the front door and go exploring. We were always going down to the waterfront to dive and fish and surf. It's actually quite cold in Tassie, but I don't ever remember it being cold as a kid. My mom said we'd come back from surfing and would be blue and she'd ask, "How was it?" And we'd say, "It was awesome!"

There was a golf course down the road from us that was quite high-end, and we used to run across it and go diving for golf balls, then sell them back to the course for money to buy fish and chips.

I don't really remember schoolwork so much, but I definitely remember having our morning tea break, and we would all jump into the kitchen and just start experimenting and baking and trying to come up with new things to eat. We used to make cakes, cause there was never anything pre-bought, and we always liked cooking with sugar. Cooking started as a bit of an escape from schoolwork, which I didn't really like. I just loved being outdoors.

My dad's family, the Glovers, are Merino wool sheep farmers up the east coast of Tasmania. So I kind of grew up there as a kid, going up for holidays, and we'd stay in the shearers quarters and go hunting on their property. Then we'd go up the coast to go surfing, and just had this lifestyle from a very young age. I guess you take it for granted when you don't know anything different.

Later, I moved away from home, and went to culinary school and started to become a chef when I was 16. It was like very traditional cooking, all about the French style of cooking, very perfect. Everything was indoors.

KM— *Where did you go to culinary school?*

SG — I went to an institution called Drysdale, a TAFE Institute here, which is like a public kind of culinary school run by the government. That's how they structured culinary school in Australia back then. My mom recognized that I liked cooking and that I was good at it. My friend's mom was the head of Drysdale and asked, "Why don't you come to chef school here?" I really loved the tactile experience.

I worked in a little restaurant after, and we had an amazing chef who was very passionate about good-quality produce — he cooked really well. He would use lots of different types of game meat that not a lot of chefs really used at the time. I remember peeling ox tongues, and frying baby sardines that they catch here in Tassie, and quail and pigeon and duck and kangaroo. I got exposed to a lot when I was really young. Then I actually left when I was 21 to become a dietician and nutritionist, because I saw this disconnect between what people were eating and their health. So I went to study at university in Queensland because I wanted to experience something different.

It didn't last very long, because my mind is more creative. I'm really glad, because I would have been stuck in a hospital and that would have been boring. So I moved to Sydney and I ran a cookie company. I did it because I wanted to be able to surf, so I lived in Bondi, surfed and made cookies from scratch.

Then I started traveling to New York for a period of four years on-and-off, because I sort of fell in love with America. I was dating a guy there at the time, and long story short, I had a restaurant in New York for a while. Later I moved back to Tasmania, and that's when I realized how I loved being out in nature, how special what we had here on the Island was. I fell back in love with my childhood and the way I grew up cooking and adventuring.

I wrote my cookbook *Wild Adventure*; that book is based on things I would do in my spare time. I just got really passionate about showing people what amazing resources we have at our fingertips — if we are willing to get our hands dirty. I set it up in a way that was inspiring to people to try and create for themselves, from practical recipes.

KM — *You now have a cooking school as well as a catering business — tell us about that.*

SG — I have a catering business called the Wild Kitchen where I cook off-grid, over open fire, using local produce from the area. I cook a lot of whole animals, use a lot of deer, and I try to use a lot of invasive species and things like that as well. In Tasmania, we're allowed to kill wallabies because there's so many of them. We also have a problem with fallow deer on the Island, which are an introduced species.

And yeah, I also do workshops to teach people to cook. They're mostly around Australia right now because of the lack of travel during the pandemic. I just try to give people a hands-on experience with cooking over fire, using whole cuts of meat, teaching a bit about butchery; teaching them how to cook protein in a way that's outside the frying pan.

I've just written a kids adventure cookbook that's coming out in April, 2021, and that's a spinoff called *Wild Child*. I also did a kids workshop — we have a local fish here called flathead, and it's really sweet eating, it's delicious. I don't think the kids had ever seen an actual flathead, and so I made them truss and stuff whole fish on little sticks, and then cooked them by the fire. They seemed so tormented, and said, "I think we're all vegetarian now." I asked them, "Where do you think your fish came from?" They loved the activity of cooking it and stuffing it by the fire, but then when it came to eating it… it was really funny, because they didn't quite know how to approach it. They're just used to getting it presented as a beautiful filet. And now they're thinking, how do I navigate through its skin and its face?

KM — *Teaching kids to cook, that's such a unique tactic. What made you decide there was a gap that needed to be filled?*

SG — For me, as a child, our family memories were built around going hunting or fishing, or we would do an activity together that was in nature. When I lived in New York and Sydney, I started to see kids whose adventure was going to a cafe and their activity was playing with an iPad. There's so much disconnection now; people aren't creating memories in nature anymore. You don't remember the meal you had at a cafe the same way you remember going fishing with your dad, or having a meal with your family.

So I just got really passionate about teaching kids as well as adults to create memories together around food, and to know how to plan their adventures. We grew up as kids who would run down or ride our bikes to the store to check the newspaper for the weather forecast, just to see if there was surf or what we could do, you know?

I'm so well-trained in checking the weather now and predicting how things are going to happen, that I can plan my adventure around that. Nowadays most kids don't know how to do that, sometimes to the point where it's dangerous. Sadly there was a local kid here that went kayaking when a huge storm came. And he died, and I thought, *Surely you would have checked the weather forecast.* There is such a disconnection now to being able to build awareness around things like the weather and nature and the food we source. So I guess my passion is showing people this through my workshops.

KM — *That's really incredible. The theme for the issue is resilience, and I feel like this speaks to that — a need for self-sufficiency — and of being aware of where we're placed in the world. What do you think are the most important life skills for people to learn from these workshops?*

SG — I think being confident with handling a fish or a bigger cut of meat. I think people just lose confidence because we've sort of grown up under the idea of perfectionism, and don't want to try things because they don't want to fail. So it's breaking it down and making it accessible. I think there's a respect that you end up having for your produce as well. Not everyone can go and catch their own seafood or fish every day, but it's great for them to feel confident when they go to the butcher or the fish market — they will have a greater awareness and appreciation for the life that was taken.

KM — *That's so important. What's been the best part of this cooking journey for you?*

SG — The moments you gain a connection with people and the places I get to go. I think everything needs to come back to community, because it's such an amazing gift that we have. I feel, in this day and age, we've become very disconnected from it because of social media, and we just end up sitting on our phones, looking at things that we don't commit to actually having.

I wouldn't have written my cookbook, *Wild Adventure*, if it hadn't been for people opening their homes and giving me boats and lending me islands and different things. The book, and what I do, wouldn't have had the spirit that it has if it wasn't for people. I think we need to get away from consumerism and appreciate human life, and know that life in general is such a gift.

KM — *That's an incredibly powerful message to bring people through food. What do you think has been the most difficult part of this?*

SG — I think stepping out of what the normality is can be lonely at times. Choosing to forge your own path can be isolating, and having enough guts to believe in your vision, and not being derailed by other people's views. I would never do what I'm doing if I had listened to everybody else; I would have just stayed in the kitchen with the metal benches and not have stepped outside of that to risk failure.

KM — *When you host these catering events, what has been the public response to you using food sourced via hunting?*

SG — It's funny, because I grew up in a family that hunts, and Tasmania is an island of farming. So it's only lately I have seen pushback when posting a couple of things about me hunting on social media. It surprised me. I've grown up doing this my whole life. I didn't really think twice that it was abnormal. Recently, when I went hunting, I posted a photo and I lost 1,200 followers.

It's just this huge detachment that we've got, because it's not normal anymore. I guess with what I do, it's like, "Hey, I'm just trying to live true to who I am and show that this is actually normal; salami's from a pig that has been killed and gutted." You should be admired for the fact that you would take the time out to do this, and find a wild resource and use it sustainably. This is the way it has been since the foundations of time. But, you know, with what I do, they either love it or hate it.

It's not just about meat for me, though. I've had vegetarians hire me for their wedding and they love what I do. So I catered a vegetarian menu for them, and I'm totally happy to do that because vegetables are amazing! My great-grandparents were carrot farmers, and it's hugely important to me where things are sourced from. And that education needs to happen. So when I'm catering, people love to watch and ask questions, and I encourage it. I encourage people to talk to us. That does require more energy, but our catering is a labor of love.

KM — *What's your favorite species to hunt?*

SG — My favorite species? Well, in Tasmania, we only have fallow deer and kangaroo, and rabbit — you have way more than we do! That's about it for getting meat in Tasmania. On the mainland, we have wild pigs and goats and different varieties of deer. I haven't been exposed to that a lot, because I just haven't had the opportunity, which is why I am super excited to come to the States and learn more.

I've actually just gotten into duck hunting here; my uncle has a marsh and we have four species of duck we can kill there. Being on an island, it's just so different. We don't have as much, but we do have incredible seafood. So I dive a lot, for crayfish and every type of fish you can imagine — it's a lot of fun.

KM — *Do you have a favorite dish for introducing people to wild game?*

SG — I quite like just cooking meat over fire, hanging it and smoking it for a long time while basting it in ghee. Keeping it simple, I'll serve it with a herb-infused oil or something I might make. We cook a lot of kangaroo in this way. I like doing it in a way where you actually taste the meat. I also love making kangaroo tail curry, which is really good as well. And then I've been loving the results of marinating venison in whiskey and pepperberry — that's a native pepper tree that grows here in Tasmania and is a bit sweeter. After dry-aging the meat for a couple of weeks, I stick it in the marinade, and into the fridge for 48 hours, then cover it in foil and slow cook it for six hours in the Traeger with olive oil. It's so good when you pull it off the bone.

KM — *Where do you find inspiration for some of these recipes of yours?*

SG — I've been interested in the cooking of Magnus Nilsson, who's quite a famous chef from the Faroe Island. They still hunt whales there, and his book includes recipes for whale blubber. It's so interesting, because on a lot of these islands, they have hunted the same way for centuries. They have these old ways of cooking things, and I wanted to learn their methods; these old women cook under the ground and they use all these different herbs and spices and techniques that I think we could learn a lot from.

There's just so much to learn from these countries. For example, countries that have super brutal winters, and the way they used to preserve and keep meat. And I think we can modernize it as well, but I do think there's something to be learned from it.

KM — *What's the wildest place you've ever cooked?*

SG — I would have to say Tasmania — it's such a wild island. Honestly, you can have five seasons in one day. But being on the top of Tassie on Flinders Island was probably the wildest. We took a boat out to where they harvested mutton birds, just how they used to do it back in the '70s. We pulled them from their burrows on the beach, which was pretty cool. It's incredible, but they're very gamey.

SARAH GLOVER — STEFAN HAWORTH

KM — *What's the wildest item in your kitchen?*

SG — The wildest item in my kitchen would have to be the machete given by my friend, Juan, who is a chef from Argentina. Everyone needs a machete.

KM — *What's the wildest recipe you've tried?*

SG — Probably kangaroo heart — pretty crazy, but it's also surprisingly delicious. I have an indigenous friend, and he and his son go hunting and they actually clobber kangaroos because it's their tradition and their culture. He was telling me they eat the heart while it's still beating, which just sounds brutal. His four-year-old son loves it. Little too hardcore for me.

I really enjoy hunting though. I like the process and the thrill you get from it. Although hunting itself can be hard, I think it's even harder preparing, storing and looking after the meat afterward. I love to hunt obviously, but I think I like to cook it more, because I like the challenge of trying to do something new with the meat.

KM — *Are most of your workshops and catering events in Tasmania?*

SG — Yes! Next year I'm actually planning to do a bit of a tour over in America, which I'm excited about.

I think what's quite interesting is that the history of Australian cuisine is very young. The Brits came in and, besides the indigenous culture, which is the Maori way of cooking over fire and under the ground, we don't have a very rich history of a certain style of cooking. It is very raw in terms of meat and veggies. We are lucky to have such a rich ecosystem here with incredible produce, because we don't have a huge population and we've got amazing resources in the land here.

---

*Visit **modernhuntsman.com** to try more of Sarah's recipes in your own wild kitchen.*

Recipe by SARAH GLOVER *Photos by* STEFAN HAWORTH **SERVES 6**

ROO ROAST *{ with Red Wine Mushrooms }*

INGREDIENTS

1	Kangaroo or wallaby leg
2	Cups ghee
250g	Mushrooms, sliced
150ml	Red wine
–	Pinch of grated nutmeg
–	Small handful of flat-leaf parsley, chopped
–	Pinch of freshly ground black pepper
–	Salt

INSTRUCTIONS

Light your fire and let it burn down for about an hour until you obtain a medium heat. Set up a tripod over the fire.

Grab the roo leg and tie some string about the knuckle. Hang it over the fire and roast for 2 hours, basting with ghee every 15 minutes to add fat – the leg is a very lean cut of meat. I like mine to be medium (if you have a meat thermometer it should be about 70C / 158F).

While the roo is cooking, place the mushrooms in a pot with 1 cup of water and bring to the boil.

Add the wine, nutmeg, parsley and pepper, and season to taste with salt. Let it boil for 2–3 minutes until slightly reduced and thickened. Set aside until the meat is cooked.

Remove the roo from the heat and let it rest for 20 minutes, then slice and dress with the warm red wine mushrooms.

SEAM *of the* SEA

Story by BETHANY GOODRICH

In Southeast Alaska, we are isolated. All 32 communities spotted across the islands of the Inside Passage are accessible only by boat or plane. Sewn to one another and the lands that sustain us, the fabric of interdependence here is a rarity that breeds resilience. Whether Indigenous or newcomer; carpenter, fisherman, politician, land manager, artist, teacher or homeless; Southeast Alaskans share a common thread woven to the nuances of land and sea. For the Tlingit, Haida and Tsimshian people, the depth of that relationship extends over 10,000 years.

IN PURSUIT OF SEALS

Though you wouldn't guess it at first glance, Robert Miller is a tailor. A literal giant — at 6'8" and nearly 300 lbs, he rivals the ancient spruce and hemlock trees that rise above our shore. In his day job as a fish biologist with the United States Forest Service, Rob helps to manage over 15,000 miles of salmon streams that pulse through the Tongass National Forest. He specializes in fish habitat enhancement, using dynamite and complex construction to stimulate wild salmon populations by increasing access to suitable spawning habitat.

Over the past eight years, I've watched Rob grow his side-hustle, Sea Fur Sewing, from humble beginnings into a prosperous business making hats, mittens, wallets and more out of Alaskan animal hides. What I've always loved about my enormous friend is the complexity of his character. He dons waders while working with the feds, camo on a moose hunt, and sweats while running his sewing machine. He's Kiks.ádi Tlingit, an entrepreneur, and arguably, a fashion designer. As a family man, he spoils his daughter with gifts of impossibly soft sea otter fur.

Rob is passionate about using his business to introduce Tlingit culture to a wider audience, and so he eagerly accepted this opportunity to share the full process of his passion, from harvest to hat. To start, we head out into Sitka Sound in pursuit of harbor seals.

The breeze moves across the aluminum skiff and lifts the grays of the covid beard Rob's been grooming since March. Both tragedy and promise swirl around the boat while we speak earnestly about the ways the pandemic has impacted our remote community, our colleagues, our families. We discuss lives lost and lives taken. Floating silently, we let the magnitude of the past seven months weigh heavy on us.

Eventually, Rob breaks the silence.

"The ocean is part of my soul. If I don't have the ocean, I feel depleted. Getting back to my roots, hunting is what I love. It's like therapy."

Honey-colored mist lifts off the ocean, crawls through the trees, and slips down the alpine spines of Baranof Island. We scan the water for the characteristic dark heads and deep eyes of harbor seals. There are endless pockets of possibility tucked into the corners, inlets, and bays of our islands. Southeast Alaska has more coastline than the rest of the United States combined. The intricacies of the Tongass National Rainforest can keep you rapt for as long as you let them. At 17 million acres, this is America's largest national forest. These public lands are also the unceded territory of the Tlingit, Haida and Tsimshian, who have honored this rainforest since time immemorial. Living as a Kiks.ádi Tlingit and working for the United States Forest Service, Rob understands the complexity of land 'ownership' deeply.

Rob proudly points out a river mouth where, years earlier, he installed a fish pass. The sun breaks above the contours of our mountains and the morning rain is soft.

Seals aren't easy to hunt. To take one demands absolute accuracy, because although harbor seals may weigh nearly 300 pounds, only the crown of their head teeters above the waterline. They rarely haul out, and are easily spooked. Arching their necks, our harbor seals sink silently in trepidation below the hinge of the horizon without making so much as a ripple. A careful headshot is necessary, ending life quickly and humanely.

We spot a pair of seals corralling coho salmon on their return to the river mouth before traveling upstream to spawn. This frenzied feast draws birds, bears, seals, eagles, maggots, and more — all sustained by the reciprocity of returning salmon. While deeply poetic, the season also reeks like death and decomposition.

Our wake startles the seals. They scatter. We move in this way for the early hours of the day, snacking, chatting, letting the angled autumn sun warm our faces.

Under the Marine Mammal Protection Act, individuals who are one-quarter Coastal Alaskan Native by blood are permitted to harvest harbor seals and other marine mammals. Blood quantum is a contentious policy that defines a sharp boundary between 'Native' and 'Non-Native,' leaving Rob on one side and his children on another. Some fear that this arbitrary cutoff threatens the long-term sustainability of this culturally-revered practice.

While Sitka is my home, I will always be a visitor on Lingít *Aaní* (Tlingit land). The concept of stewardship stretching backward and forward over ten thousand years, anchored to this abundant shore, is a relationship I'll always admire but never fully understand. As I see it, one of my responsibilities as a white person on this land is to listen to my Indigenous friends, learn about the ways colonization continues to permeate across our society, and use whatever power I have as an ally to help dismantle systems of deep-seated oppression while cultivating community resiliency. Throughout this journey, I've learned countless lessons thanks to the generosity of many mentors and peers, including Rob. One of the earliest lessons of my Southeast Alaskan education came from a colleague, Adam Davis, who gently schooled me on John Muir. When Muir came to Alaska, he denigrated the Indigenous people and excised them from their homelands in Glacier Bay. He looked down upon the seal hunt and rocked the canoe right when his Tlingit guide was about to strike. "He literally took food from our mouths," Adam explained, counting the reasons why 'conservationists' and their revisionist history aren't always welcomed in these parts.

BETHANY GOODRICH

I accidentally rock the boat while shifting in my seat to take a photo. Rob misses his first shot and we move on. I still have a lot to learn.

"I don't feel terrible about harvesting, because I think we are all predators," Rob says. "Animals are predators, the animals I harvest are predators, you and I are predators. Humans are predators to other things — our own selves mainly," he laughs. He's right.

Rob may call himself a predator, but this morning he's munching on a rice krispies treat while two seals circle around a rocky point. He pulls the skiff to shore, not taking any more chances with me on board. The shot echoes and the seal's life is over in an instant. Rob motions to run back to the skiff. Unlike sea otters with their dense and buoyant carpet of fur, seals sometimes sink, so we rush to the mushrooming blood to ensure we don't lose sight of it.

Despite our hurried efforts, the seal sinks. Rob throws anchor and grabs his fishing pole equipped with a grappling hook to hoist the animal from the sea.

Critics have many unwarranted opinions about the contemporary methods Rob and other Indigenous hunters use. No, Rob doesn't use a harpoon or a club to take seals by canoe. Relegating Indigenous people to be static, judging the nobility of their pursuits based on the tools they use, banishing them not to adapt as if imprisoned as invariable wax sculptures in some drafty museum, is just one of the many ways misconceptions of the past continue to poison the American psyche today. Rob is an Alaska Native. He uses a rifle. He uses Facebook too — not only to market his products to clients, but also to share his seal meat with eager elders across town.

Eventually the grappling hook catches into the sunken seal's flesh and Rob carefully motions the enormity of the animal to the surface before hoisting it onboard by its flippers. The seal's whiskered face leans over the edge, its blood returning to the sea. I become transfixed. The blood is intense in its brilliance — the shapes, the quantity, the vibrance, which is the very definition of red. Sealmeat is so dense with iron, pregnant women have locally coveted the meat to stave off anemia for thousands of years.

Harbor seals are variegated, ranging in shade from inky black to silver dappled in spots. This one shifts from a white belly to a black back in a ravishing, mercurial gradient. I imagine what beautiful hats Rob will one day craft from this hide. For now, he starts by honoring the meat. Carefully, Rob slices down the belly of the animal, revealing the thick sheath of blubber that insulates its violet flesh.

"Being Tlingit, for me, is just about the love for nature. You aren't wasting anything. Everything has a use. You need to share your knowledge and share your wealth — like the meat you get from the seals, you are helping the elders every chance you get. That's a core value. Do everything sustainably, because in our

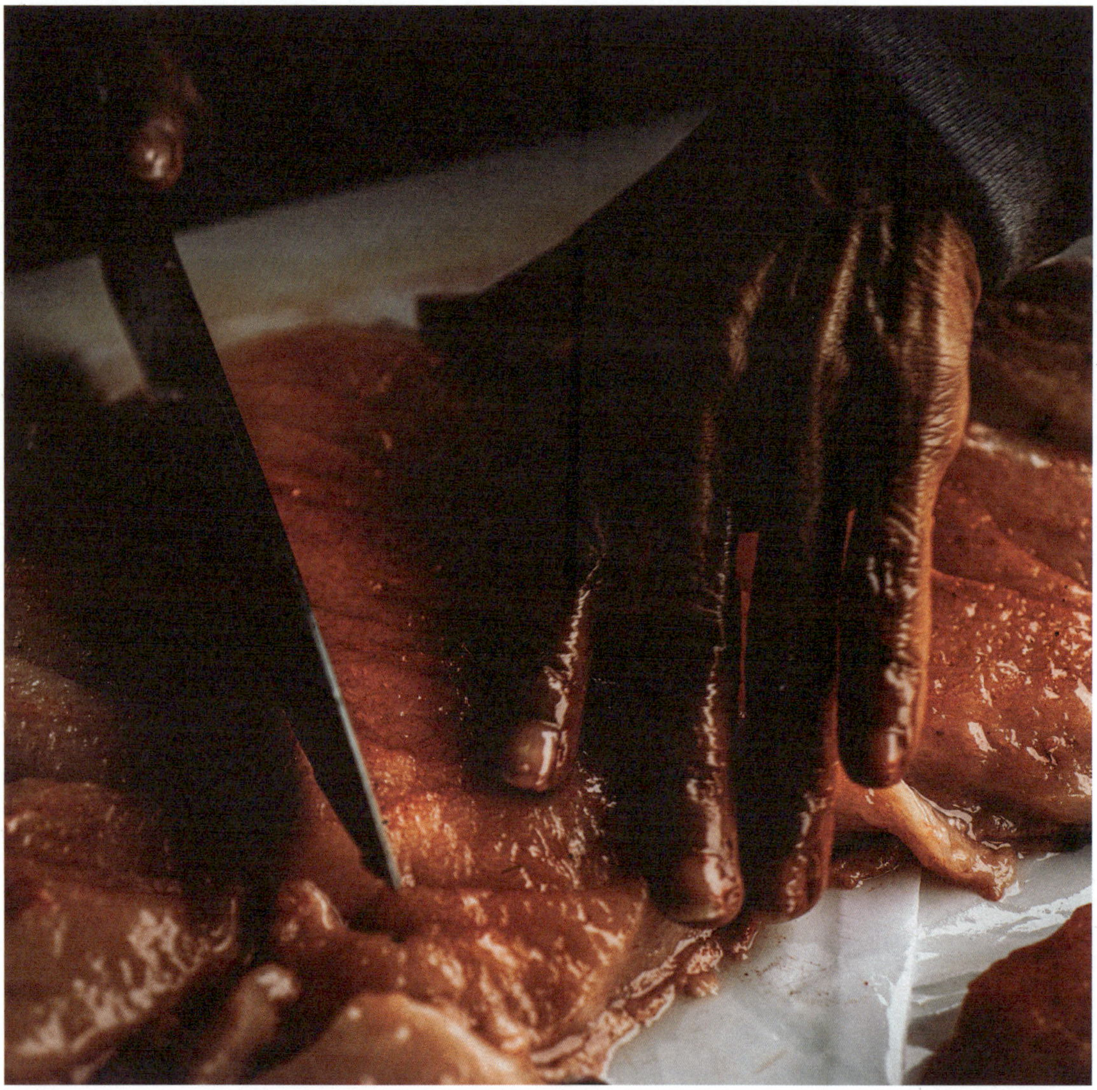

culture, Mother Earth is your number one priority. If she's not there to take care of you, it's scary."

To date, he's shared over 1,500 pounds of seal meat with individuals and institutions like our community hospital, whose Traditional Foods Program recognizes the role cultural foods play in healing.

"I need the fur, and I can bring the material back to town and make one Facebook post and give away five whole seals in twenty minutes. People aren't just hungry for anything — it's a traditional food that nobody can get anymore."

SHARING SUSTENANCE

Rob's physical opposite, Joni J. Elisoff, is waiting for us in town. She's five feet tall with small, sharp hands and she has been eagerly waiting to get them on a seal. Rob hangs the corpulent body from the rafters of his carport; Joni and I help heave the animal right below the stars and stripes of our nation's flag. The American dream takes many shapes. Rob skins the seal carefully with the rocker of an ulu knife. His neighbors cruise past slowly.

Joni hides behind a hat and hood. She's a bit bashful before the camera but also grateful for the opportunity to share something sacred to her with the world. I've never met a happier stranger. She's giddy and vivacious, floating from task to task with a fierce dedication to the process. "My Tlingit name is Kaayistann; it means friendly person." She looks up to me with a grin.

I ask her to describe the happiness she is so clearly experiencing. She pauses."The only thing I can equate it to is the joy of holding a new baby grandchild." I believe her.

The skin of Joni's hands, gleaming in oil, is so impossibly thin that I watch the bones of her fingers dance across the hills of blubber she prepares to render into oil and cracklings. We talk about health, the pandemic, and the ways she's increasingly leaning on traditional foods and remedies to cultivate vitality. A few years back, Joni started keeping the bones in her packed salmon to increase her calcium levels and mitigate the aches of osteoporosis. She sips seal oil to quell heartburn and proudly announces the positive lab results she received this week that corroborate what she already feels to be true. "It's working. I equate it all to the seal oil, to our Native foods."

Processing takes days. I visit Joni's home and gift a jar of my wild blueberry jam. Sharing food is the foundation for friendship. With each hour, Joni warms and softens like the seal blubber she stirs in an enormous pot over her stove. She shares more thoughts and more stories, including her first memories of seal. As a little girl, she and her siblings kept a seal pup they pulled from the belly of an animal her father hunted for meat. They kept it alive for days in the bathtub. She describes summers spent in her childhood cabin, putting up food, taking baths in the tidepools, preparing 'stinkheads' at low tide. Stinkheads are a wild fermentation of salmon. "We buried the heads in gunny sacks at low tide and let them go for a week and then dug them up and ate them right there on the beach. My mouth is starting to water just thinking about it. Once you get it past your nose, it tastes so good."

The seal oil is surprisingly delicate. Over low, careful heat, Joni stirs the browning bits of blubber with a loving and discerning commitment. Ladle by ladle, she spoons the golden ambrosia into mason jars throughout the day. In her little kitchen, this little lady works with every detail laid out just right for long days of processing. Autumnal gales slip inside her cracked window, lifting the embroidered butterflies of her curtains. The wind settles across the braided seal intestines she has staged for the smokehouse.

I scrub the steel smokehouse racks and Joni stokes the alder chips until steady swirls of smoke slip through cracks in the old wood walls. Into the smoker goes the meat, the ribs, and the braids of seal intestines that hang like garlands. "I know my mom is smiling," she says.

It becomes clear that Joni has poured over my informal questions with the diligence of a school student. She cares earnestly about sharing the significance of this act and sits me down with a mug of tea after another night of inward thinking. She wants another chance to articulate her joy and the reasons why processing seal matters so much to her. "The reason why it makes me so happy is it reminds me of my mother," she says. In near tears, Joni describes the smell of her childhood home and the busyness of a big family. "My mom was always putting up food."

She continues, "The other reason why it makes me so happy is I'll be able to share with my friends and family." Sharing is a foundational value in Tlingit culture. Power, unlike in a capitalist society, is not attained by how much wealth you accumulate, nor what you can claim as your own. Joni explains how power and worth is determined by how much you give away.

"My really good friend and cousin was just diagnosed with breast cancer, and all she wants is Native food as she goes through chemo. So I just sent a package off to her; that's what it's all about. It's about sharing."

By the final day, the hat and hood come off. Joni shows me the sealskin earrings she put on this morning for the pictures with pride and swings open the smokehouse door. The alder smoke pierces our eyes and contorts our smiles. My new friend beams so unabashedly, so proudly, so damn happily, all the woes of 2020 lift away with the ribbons of smoke.

LEARNING HOW TO SEW A SKIN

For some, traditions of hunting, processing and craft pass naturally, effortlessly, as an inheritance between generations.

For others, the process can be a bit more messy. Brains, bravado and a healthy dose of humility were quite literally blended together in Rob's case. "Best not to use the family blender though." His laugh fills the humble basement shop where he sews his products. Each animal has enough brains to tan its own hide. When Rob was first starting to hunt marine mammals, he wanted to try the traditional brain-tanning process too. After an argument at home, he headed out to the ocean for therapy. He took his first two otters that day, and a hunter in town showed him how to properly skin the hides.

BETHANY GOODRICH

Alaskan Fur
seafursewing

Next, it was time to tan them, so he removed the brains and into the family blender they went. His wife was horrified, catching him quite literally red-handed. "She ended up with a much nicer replacement blender," he assures me with a little grin.

Rob believes he was compelled to first start on this journey by his great grandmother's spirit. She was a seamstress and entrepreneur herself, selling seal skin moccasins to Russians and visitors in Sitka. I ask if he feels the skills and talents came naturally. He laughs again.

"I think there is a muscle memory through generations and families. There may be a little in there in my case; I think my great-grandmother is smiling. But none of it is easy if you want to be a professional and sew stuff like this — I'm exhausted every single day. Every single day I learn something. Sewing these skins together, it's a nightmare with dander flying everywhere. But it's a labor of love."

The classic Bonis fur sewing machine loops confidently through the seal hide. It's truly a stunning piece of machinery, built like a tank for delicate operations. Over years of careful diligence, Rob has mastered the idiosyncrasies of this machine. Trial and error are his predominant method. Fur sewing across the world, Rob discovered, is a secretive craft of knowledge hoarding which is so drastically unlike the culture of compassion he shares with the local Tlingit artist community.

"You're going to pay a hundred thousand dollars for some college course in Europe to learn how to sew fur." That was never an option for Rob. "So I don't even know if I'm doing it right, because I've never been taught. I am just doing it how I know. But it seems to be working. It's been a challenge every single day, but I enjoy challenges. I get bored if I am not challenged."

He lays out the templates he's designed for hats of all shapes, gloves, headbands and more. His seal and otter hats are now celebrated by people like four-time Iditorod champion Lance Mackey. They've been featured with friend Jesse Holms on shows like *Life Below Zero*, and importantly, they are most cherished locally.

"Nine years ago, I wouldn't even imagine sewing anything. Now it's become a big part of my life. I didn't even know how to thread a needle."

Unlike the uppity, knowledge-hoarding fur sewers that frustrated Rob when he began to learn this craft, he prioritizes sharing. "I've come a long way from my very first sea otter. Now I can teach others, and that's my way of giving back to my culture: by helping people learn and understand they can make money doing this too. Natives help other Natives to succeed, even as entrepreneurs."

Economic self-reliance breeds confidence and pride. "The Tlingit are proud people. Teaching people makes me feel like I'm furthering that pride. When you are able to do your art and make money at it and help your family and friends, it boosts your confidence, and that's contagious. That's where I see that going. If you can help 10 people in a community learn how to do something that they love to do, then they are going to be passionate about it and they are going to teach 10 people. It's contagious, and that's what I like. I want to see people succeed."

A COMMUNITY HUNT

This one seal stitched together a community, manifesting as food, art and economy — Joni, Rob, myself, all the people receiving shipments of oil, the people who will buy the hats, the readers of this story, Joni and Rob's ancestors. Very few places on the planet are capable of such vast and useful transcendence.

We live on the seam of the sea, where the mountains shatter as islands into the Pacific. We test the integrity of this tapestry by the strength of our returns, the character of our community and our ability to share. It's the resilience of this tapestry that shields us from the endless rain that defines our forest, the darkness of a Northern winter, or the global pandemic and economic hardship lapping at our shores. It's the resilience of this tapestry that allows us to not only survive on the islands of the Inside Passage, but to thrive.

Bethany is also Ecotrust's 2020 Rural Reporting Fellow, which is a fellowship that supports rural journalists in the West and Alaska. For more info, or to apply yourself, visit: ***ecotrust.org/project/rural-reporting-fellowship***

BETHANY GOODRICH

Illustrations by DANI VERGES *Curated by* JACK EVANS

A LETTER

As the final, glowing embers of life fade to the eternity of darkness, it is only the stories that remain. Based on undeniable truths, or figments of fiction, we shape our view of the world both from the experiences of our own lives and the fragments of those that came before. In the following pages, we present a gateway to a world forged from the past, built in the present, and projected to the future. These stories stand alone, to be embraced for their insights into human existence. It is only by exploring the thoughts of others that we can understand the motives that shape the planet we share.

Author ANONYMOUS

Dear Son,

It's Mother's Day, and there is a Wolf's hair floating in my coffee.

I have been wearing it on my sleeve all day.

Yesterday, I killed a big, white, Female Wolf.

I had wanted it to be a Male Wolf, but it wasn't.

So now it's Mother's Day and I'm thinking about Romulus and Remus and my own Mother.

She died two years and two weeks ago.

A week out here on the ice, constantly looking for tracks, everything becomes a sign.

Thoughts start to turn on you, and then begin to eat each other, 'til you're left with just sunburn, windburn, the constant ringing in your ears and a feeling of impending snow blindness.

Your eyes get weary of trying to translate immensity to your brain and then the brain starts its own crazy shit.

I'm sitting on a black lava rock island surrounded by Arctic sea ice.

Frozen Oceanic.

Baking in the heat waves.

Wearing the same clothes for nine days.

Yesterday I slept in a deserted plywood house in a town where the Inuit had been "government relocated" to someplace "with jobs."

I guess their previous jobs — nomadic hunting, fishing and trapping — ran out, although that, and snowmobiles, are all anybody really cares to talk about.

A couple of days before, I was in a survival shelter with ten more Inuit.

Some slept in the shelter with our hunting party.

Some slept in two canvas tents they traveled with.

It was about ten below zero F.

They were headed to Cambridge Bay for "Spring Frolic Festival" and the snowmobile races.

A Sled Dog was tied for the night to a snowmobile. The Dog seemed used to guarding the 800cc robot that had displaced him.

The shelter showed all the signs of humanity the next morning: frozen turds, plastic tampon applicators and uneaten ramen noodles frozen in a wad onto the ice, piss stains all over the snow.

They say the Inuit have no concept of time.

I disagree.

I think they feel the loss of it just like everybody else.

Back in the Government Ghost Town there was a hull of a Hudson's Bay Company Store that later became a native co-op, and after that a "government services" building.

It was full of unsold light bulbs, air fresheners and self help books. Also, all the files and school records of the previous generation had been spilled out onto the floor from an overturned file cabinet.

There is an unopened safe that's been drug out into the middle of the floor for walkaround inspection — like a wolf might dig out a trap.

My guide, Sam, who is the same age as me, speaks excellent but clipped English.

Inuit pronounce "No" like a baby repeats the word.

"Nnno!"

He said that when he was sent off to school the Nuns would slap him in the face with a ruler every time he said something, until he eventually figured out that he was being slapped for asking "Why are you hitting me?" in his own language.

He said he listened harder but didn't say so much after that.

He is still a very reserved man.

Sam says all of the self help books on the floor are for the young people to read so that they might cope with depression.

I think about picking up the one on obesity.

It's titled "The Kid Slimming Book."

He says I can have it if I want it.

I told him I probably wouldn't read it this late in life, and then it would just be a depressing reminder on my bookshelf.

He agreed.

He said there's a lot of depression with the young people, lots of pot, and prescription drugs and alcohol.

He told me about how last year, about this time of year, (Mother's Day?) a 25-year-old man called his Mother in Yellowknife and said he wanted to come home to her.

She arranged for him to get a free ride back with some people she knew that crewed the "Life Flight Plane" from Cambridge Bay.

When the pilot announced that they had reached cruising altitude of twenty-five thousand feet the boy opened the door and jumped out.

They never found his body.

Sam said the Bears, Wolves and Wolverines carried it off.

Sam said that when he was young most people died from botulism.

The Goose eggs they used to collect freeze and re-thaw better than government-supplied chicken eggs.

In all these abandoned buildings children have drawn on the walls with crayons and markers.

I find it odd that they are all drawing the exact same thing. They draw the stacked rock Inuit human figure cairn that you see far away in the distance.

Would-be Animists turned Anglicans by who?

God only knows.

In our hunting party is a white guy from Vancouver who drives our support sled with a hundred gallons of gas on it and all the gear we need.

We also pick up any dead sleds, parts, lost gas cans, plastic tarps and cached Caribou meat we come across.

We look like extras in a Mad Max movie.

I have a Wolverine fur hat and mirrored ski goggles and I ride in a 20-foot wooden sled that hits speeds of 60 miles per hour and sometimes catches four feet of air as we hurtle across broken sea ice, thin lake ice, eskers, crevasses, bald rock and lava gravel, usually at startling angles. The Sled probably weighs a half ton and lands like a cigarette boat on concrete.

I eat Tylenol like M&M's and position my arms like shock absorbers.

We have already turned the Sled over once but I wasn't hurt.

According to the GPS, we will crash around like that for a total of 862 miles before we're done.

My Wolverine hat and mittens have been a huge hit and every Inuit wants to try them on and take a selfie for facebook. Then they try to trade me Wolf Skin stuff for it but I tell 'em "No Way, the Wolverine is my totem animal and that's why I'm here." They're down with that, and wish me good luck on my hunt, often telling me where they have seen a particularly large Barren Ground Grizzly Bear that was "bigger than a snowmobile."

They all ask who made the hat as it has a unique style.

I tell them it was made in Alaska and that seems to make style sense to them since I'm an American.

They favor the Trapper Style hat with the turned-up brim.

My hat looks like a cross between a Wolverine and Rod Stewart.

They ask me why I have a Canada Goose Parka like theirs. Why no American Goose Parka?

I tell them that there is the Greater Canadian Goose and the Lesser Canadian Goose.

I told them the Lesser Canadian Goose was actually probably The American Goose.

So nobody wants a Lesser Goose Down Parka.

Kind of like Canadian Bacon...is better...I guess?

They liked that one and offered me some bannock in exchange for the use of my satellite phone so they could call ahead and tell their relatives in Cambridge Bay how far they were from getting home.

An elder woman squats and pees while I try to remember the country code to dial in the number for her daughter.

One day, our white-guy helper from Vancouver is wearing a Cambridge Bay Fire Department t-shirt.

I ask him if he's a fireman when he's not helping on hunts.

He said he used to be.

One night he got a call that a young girl had been drinking vodka all night and had spilled a lot of it on her shirt, and when she went to light a cigarette off the stove the shirt caught fire and burned her to death.

The address was his girlfriend's house.

When he got there it was his girlfriend's best friend.

He said he had to quit after that.

He said that since it stays light, sometimes people party for days.

My friend Thomas kills a Grizzly Bear.

ᔓ

His younger Inuit guide wants to go home now.

The next day, while he is hunting a Wolf, Sam and I see a good Grizzly Bear and give chase.

We catch him in five miles, but he is not my Bear.

He doesn't feel right.

There seems to be no need to kill him.

I watch him watch me and I call it done.

Sam knows why.

He understands.

My pal Thomas gives me the look that says: "You may have just now passed on any chance you might have had of leaving this place alive."

The next day he heads for home with his homesick guide who is missing, in his own words: his

fiancée, getting drunk, "Spring Frolic" and prescription drugs.

I go farther out on the ice.

It's all that much more serious now.

Now I'm one of "those guys." Not the worst kind — "The Trophy Hunter" — but the guy that passed on a Bear to go deeper in. It's a "heart of darkness" kind of feeling as we wind our way south down the frozen channels, now maybe 300 miles out.

About five o'clock in the afternoon, we spot a Wolverine crossing the ice.

We chase him like we do everything else, until we all get tired.

I have been blessed with seeing three Wolverines on this hunt so far.

I can't believe my own good fortune.

Until now I had only seen three in my life.

We chase the Wolverine until he's close enough, and pissed enough, to jump in the sled with me, at which point I have to stand up and make the Wolverine sign to make him "self arrest."

As much as I love looking at a Wolverine, I don't want a Wolverine lap dance.

We had heard from the Inuit headed to the races that there was an American guy on skis, pulling a sled, who was trekking across the Northwest Passage.

The Inuit thought this especially interesting because they all knew of the German that had tried the same thing a couple of years earlier.

"He had no gun but was pulling two little sleds. One in front of the other."

They could say just that in a way that translated into: "What a fucking idiot."

The German disappeared without a trace.

Sam said a Bear probably tracked him for a while and then ate him.

When we had arrived at the Ghost Town the American guy was already there in our shelter, washing his feet with hot water from his cooking pot.

His name was Peter. He was a minimalist hiker who had almost trekked all of the North American Continent.

He was from Sacramento.

He was an amazing guy, but everybody thought he was a little too minimalist when he mentioned he didn't travel with toilet paper and washed his hands and feet in the same pot he cooked in.

They thought that weird.

I reminded them that they ate the whole Caribou's face and especially loved the eyes and brains.

They still thought no TP and one pot for everything was disgusting. Besides that, the Caribou's eyes were the best part. Kind of the artichoke of a strict meat-eater's diet.

Peter reminded me of the manic reporter character Dennis Hopper played in *Apocalypse Now.*

Then I thought, That is one more sign of *"Heart of Darkness."*

He was a bit of a mad scientist and showed me several pieces of ultralight camping gear he had re-invented.

"You won't believe this," he said. "My expensive Suunto compass fucking froze! Froze!"

"I wondered if they would do that," I said.

"Why would you wonder that?"

"Because it says liquid-filled. I have a backup compass if you want it."

"Why a backup?" he asked.

"So I can check one against the other if I start to question."

"That's brilliant! I need to remember that!"

Then he took a picture of my stove.

The next day he mushed off, towing his plastic sled.

A day later some Inuit reported that they saw Bear tracks behind his.

That night of Mother's Day, the 11th, we saw large Bear tracks headed south along the right side of a huge fault line.

So we followed them, knowing that at any time, the Bear could take a left and disappear into the rocks on the island he was paralleling.

After three miles we were getting excited. The Bear had not changed course.

There is nothing more fun than sight hunting.

I was looking as far ahead as I could, and then I saw the Bear.

He was three miles away, still on the ice, but walking only a few feet from the frozen shore of a long island jutting out of the solid sea.

I knew immediately that he was my Bear.

What I did not know was whether or not I would kill him or if he would get away.

That would be God's decision.

To a hunter, an Animal is a Blessing.

The Animal is the sign of the hunting place for all of time.

Not some souvenir. The Animal is a symbol, a monument.

A sign.

A hunt can always go either way.

We closed on him for two miles, stopping often to watch him with binoculars to see if he had heard the sled yet, to see if he was looking in our direction.

When we were two miles out we unhooked the sled and I got on the back of the snowmobile.

I was holding my rifle across the seat between Sam and me with my left hand.

My right hand was clenched onto a handlebar mounted on the right side of the machine.

I knew I had just signed up for the ejection seat.

Sam immediately gave the machine full throttle. The chase was on.

We hadn't gone 300 yards before the Bear heard or maybe felt us.

The Bear looked at us, turned, started running at a full gallop, then cut left and up into the rocky cliffs and ledges of the island.

We didn't hesitate; we cut left a mile behind him and at the same speed up into slick rock, blind corner ledges and escarpment.

I thought to myself:
If you get scared you can't think straight.

Trust God.

Maybe you have to risk your life for this Bear.

This can be the only chase.

This is the only way to make it fair.

It can go either way now.

It was a mechanized version of a Buffalo Run.

I was holding my rifle like a lance, my thoughts the words to a death song. I was prepared to die on this chase and I felt the Bear was winning the chase.

I knew Sam felt the same way.

We were wild Indians.

We were wild and free.

The Bear was a thousand times greater.

I trusted everything above me.

Then we realized we had lost him.

We raced back at a sickening angle, at an awful speed.

Tracks went up and over the top, a place we couldn't possibly go without tumbling over backward.

We cut left and down, full tilt, to try and maintain a line that wouldn't carry us over a cliff.

We hit the sea just as we ran out of room.

We raced the two miles back to the sled.

Flying over the frozen waves.

Like a pit crew, we untied a gas can and filled the machine, trying to not spill gas on the red-hot engine, re-hooked the sled, and then we were off in the direction we had come, hoping, praying that the Bear might maintain flight over the top of the island and somehow come out on the sea ice on the opposite side.

We would go back and all the way around as fast as we could, just to see.

It was hope beyond hope, but it was the hope we had.

Fifteen minutes of full-speed later we rounded the tip of the island and racked the sled to a high point near the tip.

The Bear was just running out to the ice a mile away.

It was stark and silent

Sam dismounted the machine, walked out to stare at him, then came back.

In a quiet voice, he said:

"I think we have him now.

We will wait till he's farther out on the ice."

I felt sick. The Bear was singing his death song now.

He had committed.

I would have to kill him now.

Then we cut the Bear off from the shore of the island.

He was running on the ice, right to left, full tilt.

My first shot missed.

It's hard to kill something that you hate to.

I racked the bolt and shot into him.

He spun. I had shot him through the front shoulders. Then he sat down on the ice. He showed me his heart, I shot it, and he fell down.

I used the awful strength it takes to kill a Bear.

We used the rest of it we had to shake hands, to laugh, to still be hunters.

To hold each other up, high enough to see the Bear.

THANK YOU TO OUR

PARTNERS

FOR VOLUME SIX

CHRISTENSEN ARMS®

VORTEX®

TECOVAS

EPIC PROVISIONS™

FIRST LITE

MYSTERY RANCH